The New Professional

A Resource Guide for New Student Affairs Professionals and Their Supervisors

Edited by
David D. Coleman
John E. Johnson

Technical Editors
Diane J. Coleman
Sally E. Watson

The New Professional: A Resource Guide for New Student Affairs Professionals and Their Supervisors. Copyright © 1990 by the National Association of Student Personnel Administrators, Inc. Printed and bound in the United States of America. All rights reserved. No part of this book may be reproduced in any form or by any electronic or mechanical means, without written permission from the publisher. First edition.

Library of Congress Cataloging-in-Publication Data
The new professional: a resource guide for new student affairs professionals and their supervisors/edited by David D. Coleman and John E. Johnson.—1st ed.
    p. cm.
  Includes bibliographical references.
  ISBN 0-931654-12-2: $9.95
  1. College student personnel administrators—United States.
I. Coleman, David D.   II. Johnson, John E.
LB2343.N397 1990
378.1'9425—dc20   90-32308
                                                CIP

The editors acknowledge and dedicate this monograph to the following people whose encouragement and support have been gratefully appreciated: Diane, Marvin, Vivian, Gail and Karen; Ruth and Shelby; and Dr. Stanley Carpenter.

NASPA Monograph Board 1989-90

Editor
George D. Kuh
Professor of Education
Indiana University
Bloomington, Indiana

Members

Dana Burnett
Vice President for Student Services
Old Dominion University
Norfolk, Virginia

Deborah Ellen Hunter
Assistant Professor
University of Vermont
Burlington, Vermont

Michael L. Jackson
Associate Dean for Campus Affairs
Stanford University
Stanford, California

Carmen Jordan-Cox
Vice President for Student
 Development
University of San Francisco
San Francisco, California

Herman Kissiah
Dean of Students
Lafayette College
Easton, Pennsylvania

Daryl Smith
Associate Professor
Claremont Graduate School
Claremont, California

Rodger Summers
Vice President for Student
 Affairs
West Chester University
West Chester, Pennsylvania

Elizabeth J. Whitt
Assistant Professor
Oklahoma State University
Stillwater, Oklahoma

Contents

The Authors .... *vi*

Foreword
Gerald L. Saddlemire .... *vii*

Chapter 1
The New Professional
David D. Coleman and John E. Johnson 1

Chapter 2
Making the Transition to a Professional Role
Margaret J. Barr 17

Chapter 3
Using Theory and Performing Research in Everyday Practice
Roger B. Winston, Jr. 30

Chapter 4
Developmental Concerns in Moving toward Personal and Professional Competence
D. Stanley Carpenter 56

Chapter 5
A Lifestyle Approach to Stress Management
Frances T. O'Brien and Steven K. Erwin 73

Appendix
Professional Associations and Publications 84

The Authors

Margaret J. Barr, Vice Chancellor for Student Affairs, Texas Christian University, Fort Worth, Texas

D. Stanley Carpenter, Assistant Professor of Educational Administration, Texas A&M University, College Station, Texas

David D. Coleman, Director of Student Activities and Director of the University Center, Xavier University, Cincinnati, Ohio

Steven K. Erwin, Assistant Director of Housing, University of Wisconsin, Platteville, Wisconsin

John E. Johnson, Assistant Director of Student Life, University of Alabama, Birmingham, Alabama

Frances T. O'Brien, Director of Administration, National Wellness Institute, Stevens Point, Wisconsin

Gerald L. Saddlemire, Professor of College Student Personnel, Bowling Green State University, Bowling Green, Ohio

Roger B. Winston, Jr., Professor of Student Personnel and Higher Education, University of Georgia, Athens, Georgia

Foreword

Results of research on career patterns of preparation program graduates show that 25-40 percent of those graduates (Burns, 1982; Saddlemire, 1988) leave the student affairs profession within five years. The likelihood that the remaining 60-75 percent will continue in the profession is influenced by the extent to which they understand their personal and professional development, as well as what the individual and supervisor do to ensure a satisfactory experience in such development.

How can young professionals become older professionals who have not lost their enthusiasm and commitment for a career in student affairs? What are the concerns, fears, opportunities, and needs of a new practitioner starting up the career ladder in higher education? These questions have been discussed in workshops, at state and national conferences, in newsletters, and by preparation program faculty. These questions stimulated the development of this monograph.

The topics in each chapter were embraced to encourage new and seasoned professionals to reflect on the socialization process experienced by new staff members. However, a young professional's unique concerns may not remain high on individual agendas, even though everyone is (or has been) a young professional. It is hoped that senior student affairs staff members and graduate preparation program faculty will find insights in this monograph that assist in designing programs to meet the unique needs of preservice students and new full-time staff appointees. A profession that claims to be caring of students should do no less for its own professionals. Retention of staff members is as cost effective as retention of students.

The contributors to this monograph represent a balance of ideas from new professionals to well-established senior scholars. David D. Coleman and John E. Johnson set the stage for the monograph by describing certain characteristics about new professionals. The authors also discuss why collaboration is needed between supervisors and new professionals to encourage personal and professional development, and positive contributions to the supporting institutions' goals and missions.

Margaret J. Barr discusses questions that are typical of a person appointed to their first professional student affairs position. She also addresses common concerns in a transition to a new professional role and suggests appropriate strategies to confront the issues as perceived by the new professional or their supervisor(s).

Roger B. Winston, Jr., expounds upon the intricate use of theory and research in everyday student affairs practice. He encourages applying theories as the basis for practice and elaborates on various uses of theory to design effective programs and interventions on the student's behalf.

D. Stanley Carpenter describes the path toward personal excellence and professionalism while warning that each person must make choices based on his/her particular level of competence. He emphasizes that understanding one's particular institutional climate and culture is essential for intentional professional development.

According to Frances T. O'Brien and Steven K. Erwin, the demands on the young professional are often antithetical to appropriate lifestyle choices and effective stress management. By outlining sources of stress and citing coping strategies, these authors share how to make choices that are most likely to increase job satisfaction and improve personal health and effectiveness.

An appendix of professional associations and journals is included as a resource for involvement and professional affiliation. Student affairs professionals must take specific action (e.g., acquiring association membership, joining a committee, submitting journal articles) to maximize the effectiveness of the resources listed.

This monograph makes a significant contribution to the body of knowledge which currently exists about new professionals. New professionals, supervisors, and student affairs associations are encouraged to utilize the monograph as a means for fostering growth; assisting in transitions; understanding self, supervisors, and mentors; and comprehending the theories and roles of student affairs professionals.

Gerald L. Saddlemire

REFERENCES

Burns, M.A. (1982). Who leaves the student affairs field? *NASPA Journal,* 20(2), 9-12.

Saddlemire, G.L. (1988, March). Young professionals' mobility. Paper presented at the meeting of the American College Personnel Association, Miami, Florida.

Chapter 1

The New Professional

David D. Coleman and John E. Johnson

Exploring the concept of a new professional is a complex endeavor. The role of a new professional is linked to organizational structure and dynamics, an individual's commitment to higher education, self-growth, and a balance between work and personal life.

Who are new professionals? New professionals are often thought of as recent graduates in search of an entry-level position. However, they can also be at various ages and levels of education or experience. For this monograph, new professionals are defined as graduate students, professionals within the first five years of employment, or people changing disciplines within an occupation or returning to an occupation after an extended absence.

In this chapter we will examine the subject of new professionals by describing and analyzing such areas as preparing to become a new professional, the transition from preparation to practice, professional development and advancement, networking, professionalism, crisis management and conflict resolution, advancement in student affairs, and supervision and mentoring.

PREPARING TO BECOME A NEW PROFESSIONAL

Long before graduation from college, students go through the process of (directly or indirectly) selecting determinants which may influence their careers. Examples of such determinants include area of study, concentration of study within a degree field, selection of mentors, and assistantship activities. These factors all contribute to personal and professional growth, the degree of which may depend on such components as preparation, cocurricular activities, and peer-mentoring relationships. Certainly, growth may be hindered by poor preparation, inactivity or apathy as students fail to broaden their interests and skills. Later, as a new professional, the student's ability to seek greater self-awareness within the context of the working world is central to the developmental process and obtaining vocational maturity (Arnold, 1982).

Professional development might even be inhibited by graduate preparation programs if graduates feel prepared to quote newfound knowledge but unprepared to apply these ideas to real life situations. Knefelkamp (1979) observed that one cannot translate theory directly into practice. There is a critical middle step in the process: translating the theory into accurate characteristics of particular students in particular environments. Knefelkamp (1979) also believes that we cannot "develop" students. The best we can do is attempt to design environments that provide sufficient conditions so that development can be facilitated. Therefore, the new professional is challenged to actively transfer theory into practical applications which reflect environmental designs and student characteristics.

TRANSITION FROM PREPARATION TO PRACTICE

The ability to assume new roles in a positive, straightforward manner can ensure a successful transition from preparatory programs to practice. The transition is affected by such variables as the support of the institution, faculty contacts, mentoring relationships, peer support, and individual preparation and motivation.

Allen (1987) proposed six stages of professional competence that can enhance a new professional's ability to survive the transition.

- Gain knowledge by taking courses, attending workshops, or reading professional literature. New professionals can plan more effectively by following current issues and trends in student affairs.
- Understand how to apply knowledge and information. An important component of job performance is professional-client interaction. This interaction is improved by the professional's ability to apply knowledge to practical situations.
- Apply and practice knowledge and information. The new professional can build confidence by taking risks and testing abilities.
- Use a skill or knowledge with specific intent.
- Facilitate the learning or growth in others. During daily planning and problem solving, the new professional encourages fellow coworkers to learn.
- Transfer competence to others. Transferring competence can be achieved through such activities as role modeling, supervision, and performance evaluation.

These stages outline the continuity of professional development which culminates in productive and helpful relations with others. The stages also provide new professionals with a means of monitoring their own professionalism and competency. Throughout these stages, new professionals cannot lose sight of their career goals. Consider Zach's (1985) statement, "You need to be interested in the future because you are going to spend the rest of your life there." Some simple advice would be to maintain long-range (future) goals of at least five years or more to plan for prospective career development. An example of a long-range goal would be to work toward practicing and acquiring specific professional experience prior to beginning a doctoral degree program.

Short-range (current) goals of one to four years should be more specific in nature. An example of a current goal would be to attend a conference or workshop on a specialized topic (e.g., affirmative action or performance evaluation) to gain immediate knowledge, or to speak at an upcoming conference to develop presentation skills.

Goal setting, whether on a short- or long-term basis, is crucial for the new professional. Current goals can provide a basis for periodic self-evaluation and redefinition of interests. Planning current goals may also be easier for new professionals because future goals seem to be overshadowed by more immediate needs such as acceptance, peer support, and role understanding. Goals should therefore be based upon incremental, achievable experiences—moving from simple to more complex—which when realized, facilitate personal and professional growth and development (Perlmutter, 1982). However, to rest upon accomplished goals is inhibitive, for as soon as they are realized they no longer play an active role in personal and professional growth.

PROFESSIONAL DEVELOPMENT AND ADVANCEMENT

The term professional development is often misused to refer to time away from work. However, development can occur in daily work experiences during meetings with colleagues or conferences with students or parents. Professional development is defined as "a planned experience designed to change behavior and result in professional and/or personal growth and improved organizational effectiveness" (Merkle and Artman, 1983, p. 55).

Is professional development important? Leafgren (1981) observed that development opportunities for new professionals, especially residence educators, should hold a dominant position in the hierarchy of needs for supervisors and institutions. Leafgren's beliefs are based on the fact that professionals, especially residence educators, are front line personnel with students and often face greater stress and anxiety in relation to their jobs.

In structuring professional development, supervisors and institutions can address the hierarchy of needs by monitoring staff involvement and commitment to reduce burnout and increase productivity. For example, a professional entering student affairs from another discipline, or outside higher education, may have more complex needs for theory orientation than a traditional preparation program graduate with a background in theory coursework.

Professionals are wise to comprehend and internalize the institution's mission when planning their own professional development schemes. They should consider departmental priorities, funding, time commitments, and institutional support. Conflicts can occur when an individual's idea of a developmental opportunity differs from an institution's. Conflict situations may lead to unsupportive behavior in the form of placing individual priorities above the institution's, displaying a lack of concern for funding or insincere commitment to responsibilities. In reality, this unsupportive behavior might stem from a simple communication breakdown or a misunderstanding of needs, goals, or expectations between supervisors and employees.

An overlooked avenue for professional development is attending in-service programming. Stamatakos and Oliaro (1972) wrote, "In-service development is a vital method for maintaining the necessary level of information and competence to allow student personnel workers to meet the challenges of their job in an assertive, productive fashion" (p. 270). Additionally, staff members may present programs themselves to share an area of expertise.

Conference attendance can also stimulate professional development. However, a supervisor's concern might be that conferences, seminars, workshops, and presentations divert new professionals from their job responsibilities. Therefore, preparation for this type of development is important to objectively justify time and expenses. Some examples of preparation include keeping accurate travel expenses, working efficiently and effectively to complete responsibilities in advance, and making arrangements to uphold commitments upon returning to work (Knefelkamp, 1986).

Skill building can, along with collegial contact and role modeling, assist new professionals in becoming more competent, confident, and productive members of their staffs. Canon (1984) supported the interrelationships of these experiences by affirming, "In the education field, we are concerned about the [ethical] development of students. We must be equally concerned about the quality of human interaction [and development] of faculty and staff" (p. 110).

Leafgren (1981) asserted that the personal and professional growth of staff members is enhanced by establishing several premises concerning the milieu.

- Everything can be a learning experience. Evaluations with supervisors, committee involvement, or conversations with students are examples.
- There are no real failures. Failures can be valuable learning opportunities for personal and professional improvement.
- The creativity, new ideas, and talent of new professionals should be encouraged. Talented and creative new professionals stimulate growth in student affairs as they share new technologies, theories, program ideas, and solutions.
- Competencies are rewarded and [unhealthy] competition is discouraged. Young professionals should be encouraged to share their competencies rather than using them merely for individual gain or reward for "out doing" others. Competition with colleagues is healthy if carried out with mutual respect and with the desire to advance the profession and meet individual goals.
- It is professionally acceptable to experience both positive and negative emotions and be upset with others. The expression of these feelings should be encouraged as a normal human response. However, professionalism must be maintained.
- Stumbling and learning to pick up oneself gives the new professional additional courage and freedom. A crucial aspect of personal and professional growth is learning from mistakes and positively applying that knowledge to future events.

Leafgren's premise is that the major goals for developing student affairs personnel are set in the framework of specific developmental tasks and identity. The desired outcomes are personal awareness, emotional and instrumental autonomy, and actualizing a wellness lifestyle (Leafgren, 1981). Personal awareness is a major goal. Without a true sense of what they have accomplished personally and professionally, new professionals might find making a decision about the future difficult, if not impossible.

A second major goal is the development of autonomy—individuals taking responsibility for their own lives. The new professional must gain a sense of independence while simultaneously developing productive relationships with peers and colleagues.

The third major goal involves the wellness continuum in which positive decisions lead to a personal and professional lifestyle that is maximally fulfilling and rewarding. These decisions may deal with nutrition, personal relationships, and balancing work and recreation. The process is continuous, cumulative, and requires time and a belief in human potential. Wellness also includes personal development and stress management as vital lifestyle factors. Improvements in these areas can be achieved by assessing, planning, and implementing effective, lifelong, stress management techniques.

NETWORKING

Networking can be described as "the exchange of information or services among individuals, groups or institutions" (Webster, 1985, p. 794) or a collaboration between people to "get better jobs or to be more effective on the job" (Welch, 1980, p. 4). Networking is important because interacting with colleagues is inevitable and "seems to be one of the primary ways new professionals can conquer their apprehensions, minimize job anxiety, develop a support system, and promote the development of a career philosophy" (Hayman, 1984, pp. 77-78).

Networking at conferences and workshops can result in the exchange of program ideas, professional techniques, or personal beliefs. Past relationships are often rekindled in an environment that fosters personal and professional recommitment.

Perhaps the most crucial factor in networking is credibility (Dartnell, 1985):

- Be consistent and predictable in how you treat people. Coworkers and students may feel insecure when they do

not know what to expect in terms of behavior. Consistency enables others to develop plans for presenting information and ideas to you.
- Spot problems and devise solutions. Take a realistic approach to problem solving by recognizing all of the issues involved and devising a solution which addresses the priority issue(s). Represent the organization professionally and be accountable for your decisions.
- Keep your promises. Demonstrate credibility by following through on plans and programs in a timely manner. Levin (1985) equated credibility with a batting average, suggesting that each time you give false or ineffective information, your batting average will decrease along with your credibility. Your effectiveness as a leader relates to your "believability."
- Be available for advice and help. People appreciate a colleague who is accessible and supportive. While listening to others, demonstrate sincerity and empathy. Share ideas and solutions and maximize what you have learned.

By adhering to these four principles, new professionals can make effective use of networking skills that will contribute to the development of an effective interaction style.

PROFESSIONALISM

Professionalism is discussed in classrooms, workshops, and student affairs orientations; but what exactly does professionalism entail? According to Faux (1985), professionalism involves
- Being available to honor commitments in a timely and reliable manner. Although working on committees, making presentations or writing articles is admirable, these involvements are secondary to your professional role.
- Being ready by being informed and prepared to utilize what you claim to know. As Levin (1985) suggested, strive for the highest batting average of credibility possible.
- Being aware of group and interpersonal dynamics and your role within the group. Know when feedback, humor, and active listening are appropriate.

- Being in control and gaining composure to handle future situations and challenges.
- Being honest about your strengths and limitations. Give credit to others for their ideas and substantiate your work with documentation.
- Being purposeful and knowing the task at hand. Set personal and professional goals and objectives.
- Being creative and adventurous while contributing to the improvement of higher education.

A professional is one who strives for mastery of these seven basic principles.

Competition is another component of professionalism and professional development. Competition is healthy when professionals are challenged to apply theoretical knowledge, question beliefs, and evaluate personal competence and effectiveness. Additionally, competition can motivate professionals to work more closely with colleagues, learn from mentors, and pursue advanced degrees.

A discussion on professionalism would not be complete without mentioning ethics. Gaber and Haxton (1985) defined professional ethics as "a moral obligation to do what ought to be done, the study of morals and moral issues, a set of principles that serves as life's guide, and a philosophical base on which to make decisions about behavior." For guidance, professionals can review institutional mission and professional association goal statements which often contain expectations regarding ethical conduct. However, professionals must recognize that they may hold certain ethical beliefs not aspired to by the institution. For example, an activity that the new professional might consider to be hazing may be thought of as a tradition by alumni. Thus, an imperative for new professionals is to assess the congruence between values they hold sacred and ethical considerations to which the institution is committed. A large discrepancy between these two mind sets could make for an uncomfortable, unproductive work environment.

CRISIS MANAGEMENT AND CONFLICT RESOLUTION

One of the new professional's initial career challenges comes through an exposure to crisis and conflict situations. Such conflicts are often related to parental grievances, legal dilemmas, or policy issues. Several strategies to apply to these conflict situations are:

- Maintain optimism within a realistic framework. Seek out the good in people and situations, even through difficult times. In handling problems, imitate those people whose styles and strategies seem to be most effective.
- Identify all relevant facts before acting. Be cognizant that hidden agendas or past experiences may confound situations. Ignorance of even one small bit of information, such as unknowingly criticizing a colleague's program, may cause an irreversible loss of credibility. The bottom line is to choose battles wisely. "If accused of a wrongdoing or inefficiency, make absolutely sure that the correction is worth the possible animosity and self-polarization that requesting an apology or indicating the true culprit may cause" (Brodzinski, 1979, p. 9).
- Realize that not all conflict is negative. For example, a situation may arise that calls for a decision or choice between two or more positive variables.

ADVANCEMENT IN STUDENT AFFAIRS

Advancement in student affairs can be realized through formal education (graduate degrees), career growth (interviewing and changing jobs), and professional education (acquiring student development knowledge). Mable (1985) offered a perspective on what individuals can do to improve their chances for advancement in student affairs:

- Conduct a study and write a follow-up article. Develop skills in investigating and presenting issues and ideas.
- Find a caring, challenging mentor. Quality mentors encourage professionals, through support and challenge, to become contributing members of the profession.

- Be fully involved with students, staff, and the job. Be alert, visible, and enthusiastic.
- Work hard and enjoy hard! A balance between work and recreation affects positive lifestyle choices (Leafgren, 1981).
- Keep up with student affairs literature and be aware of current events in higher education. A better understanding of current student affairs issues can lead to dialogues on such topics as student retention or student involvement and academic success.
- Be able to share examples of your accomplishments.
- Become involved in a professional association. Gain practical experience and knowledge while developing significant relationships with peers.

Another way to advance professionally is to establish marketability. Marketability refers to the experiences and skills of a knowledgeable professional that can translate into preferential standing for job placement. To increase marketable skills, professionals can absorb knowledge, sharpen abilities, and become more involved with the community where they live and work (Allen, 1987).

Some degree of specific and general knowledge is desirable in student affairs. A marketable candidate sees the small picture in relation to a broad background of information. For example, a professional who can recruit students to a campus but lacks the general understanding of student housing related to retention may achieve only short-term success.

Another aspect of marketability deals with commitment and longevity. An employee who begins a position with insincere commitment and a preconceived timeframe of tenure may end up counting the days to a new job. This new professional, when faced with adversity, might feel that he/she has an escape route since he/she was leaving anyway. Although sometimes important for psychological health, the situation can provide professionals with a feeling of "one-upmanship." The employee's behavior may be seen as a lack of institutional commitment. Both parties lose because the institution does not have a completely productive staff member and the individual experiences diminished skills resulting from a lack of effort and interest.

Arnold (1982) addressed the issue of job stability by asserting that "in some circles it has become almost fashionable to change jobs or careers. One needs only to look as far as our own newly minted professionals to find a whole group who consider more than a two-year tenure in their first position as professional stagnation. When confronted with a personal crisis which stems from diminished job satisfaction, the support [that] society provides for change is particularly appealing. It is no wonder that even successful young student affairs professionals identify with the poignant question, 'Is that all there is?' and then jump ship" (p. 6).

It can be inhibiting to leave an institution with the perception that it is time to move on. However, appropriate reasons for leaving may include a feeling that no more experience or knowledge can be gained; or another position may be more attractive for financial, emotional, or professional reasons; and job candidacy is strong. In terms of longevity, Lawing, Moore, and Groseth (1982) contended that "some logical relationships exist between a person's tendency to remain in student affairs and variables thought to influence career stability. Job satisfaction, number of years, and position held in the field tend to influence a person to remain in the field. Those who expect to remain also tend to be happier in their work and tend to see their own formal education as adequate" (p. 24).

In addition to commitment, loyalty is also an issue for new professionals. Carried to its illogical extreme, institutional loyalty can be a tremendous stumbling block to an individual's career advancement. A single institution, no matter how large, simply cannot offer a complete range of opportunities. Clearly, the discrepancy between personal and institutional priorities is problematic when career advancement is at issue (Arnold, 1982).

SUPERVISION AND MENTORING

Supervision is continued interaction between an employee and a supervisor for the purpose of reaching common goals and objectives. Effective supervision is essential to the development of a new professional. The supervisor's role should be that of facilitator and resource person, challenging a subordinate to develop skills and character. However, the notion that supervisors must provide continual direction is erroneous, despite the fact that supervisors are sometimes viewed as all knowing.

New professionals can assist in their own development by being constantly alert and willing to assume the varied roles and tasks supervisors will ask them to perform. Ultimately, elicitation must give way to facilitation if the new professional is to develop an independent style.

Webster (1985) described a mentor as a "trusted counselor or guide" (p. 742). Supervisors should assume a strong role in the mentoring process because they create and control the environment in which subordinates perform goal-oriented tasks, test skills, acquire knowledge, and apply theory to practical situations. Supervisors should also resist the temptation to develop mirror images of themselves. In addition, a mentor can only assist the new professional to the limits of his or her individual potential and desire.

On occasion, a supervisor may not be the appropriate mentor for a new professional. A supervisor in an unfulfilling position can be a negative influence on new and experienced colleagues. As a result of reduced interaction with students or job stagnation, supervisors may experience a situation where institutional, financial, or collegial support outweighs professional challenge. Mable (1985) identified these people as *driftwood professionals.* Their existence often necessitates an (informal) redistribution of tasks to ensure the successful completion of goals. This often places undue stress on colleagues who may cover for them by completing job responsibilities.

Another imbalance can occur when a driftwood professional is in a supervisory position and either has no intention of advancing within the profession or has advanced beyond his or her capabilities. This scenario causes conflict when a new professional, just starting to gain experience, does not receive the direction and support he or she needs to succeed. A volatile conflict may surface when a supervisor perceives that their level of competence is surpassed by that of a staff member. These driftwood professionals need to be encouraged by students and colleagues to take a more positive approach to their careers or to relinquish their positions to someone with more creativity and energy.

Finally, supervisors and mentors can assist new professionals by sharing knowledge about human development. Supervisors and mentors sometimes do not understand, or are unwilling to discuss, human development theory. According to Heineman and Strange (1984, p. 53), 92 percent of the professionals they surveyed reported using human development theory to explain or understand individual student behavior. However, only 62 percent of the professional staff members reported discussing theory with their supervisors (Heineman and Strange, 1984). If discussion between new professionals, supervisors, and mentors is not occurring, an opportunity is missed for the new professional to analyze their comprehension and application of theoretical knowledge bases. "With the knowledge explosion experienced in student affairs over the past decade, more emphasis should be placed on such opportunities. Perhaps the findings suggest that the infusion of knowledge base into the field may be a unilateral phenomenon from the 'bottom up,' supported by those who have recently completed professional training but not actively encouraged by those in decision-making positions" (Heineman and Strange, 1984, pp. 531-32).

SUMMARY

Becoming a student affairs professional is a complex endeavor. New professionals need to begin by striving for a balance between acquired theoretical knowledge and application to practical situations. In addition, they must seek out an adequate degree of challenge and support from caring, competent peers and mentors. Supervisors play a critical role in providing this challenge and support.

New professionals must be alert and willing to assume the varied roles they will be asked to perform in their initial years.

They must exercise their skills and be patient in making assumptions about people, programs, and policies. Attitude and preparation are inextricably linked to professional success. New professionals who remain patient and strive to learn from every situation will grow into competent professionals who will provide leadership in the 21st century.

REFERENCES

Allen, K.E. (1987). Six stages of competence. In National Association of Campus Activities (Ed.), *Future prefect: A guide for professional development and competence* (pp. 9-14). Columbia, South Carolina: Author.

Arnold, K. (1982). Career development for the experienced student affairs professional. *NASPA Journal,* 20(2), 3-8.

Brodzinski, F.R. (Ed.). (1979). *The management primer: Guidelines for new professionals.* (Available from Commission I, ACPA, Alexandria, Virginia 22304).

Canon, H.J. (1984). Developmental tasks for the profession: The next 25 years. *Journal of College Student Personnel,* 26, 110.

Dartnell Corporation Bulletin (1985). Gaining credibility. Dartnell Corporation. Chicago, Illinois: Author.

Faux, R.L. (1985). On being professional. Unpublished manuscript.

Gaber, R., and Haxton, L. (1985, November). Being professional and ethical. Paper presented at the meeting of the Upper Midwest Region Association of College and University Housing Officers, Aberdeen, South Dakota.

Hayman, D.R. (1984). Life as a new professional: A personal viewpoint. *Journal of College Student Personnel,* 26, 77-78.

Heineman, D., and Strange, C. (1984). Uses of human development theory by entry-level practitioners in student affairs. *Journal of College Student Personnel,* 25(6), 528-33.

Knefelkamp, L.L. (1979). The developmental issues of graduate students: A model of assessment. Unpublished manuscript.

Knefelkamp, L.L. (1986, February). Justifying your professional development. A paper presented at the National Association for Campus Activities, Washington, D.C.

Lawing, M.A.; Moore, L.V.; and Groseth, R. (1982) Enhancement and advancement: Professional development in student affairs. *NASPA Journal,* 20(2), 22-26.

Leafgren, F. (1981). Student development through staff development. *Journal of College Student Personnel,* 28, 218-28.

Levin, A. (1985, March). Keynote address. Paper presented at the American College Personnel Association, Boston, Massachusetts.

Mabel, P. (1985, November). Consultant-in-residence with new professionals. Paper presented at the Upper Midwest Region Association of College and University Housing Officers, Aberdeen, South Dakota.

Merkle, H.B., and Artman, R.B. (1983). Staff development: A systematic process for student affairs leaders. *NASPA Journal,* 21, 55.

Perlmutter, M. (1982). Setting goals and objectives. Unpublished manuscript.

Stamatakos, L.C., and Oliaro, P.M. (1972). In-service development: A function of student personnel. *NASPA Journal,* 9, 270.

Webster's ninth new collegiate dictionary. (1985). Springfield, Massachusetts: Merriam-Webster.

Welch, M.S. (1980). *Networking.* New York: Harcourt, Brace and Jovanovich.

Zach. D. (Speaker). (1985). Futures in the world of work (videotape). Stevens Point, Wisconsin: University of Wisconsin, Stevens Point.

Chapter 2

Making the Transition to a Professional Role

Margaret J. Barr

Acceptance of a first professional position in student affairs brings with it many questions, concerns, and emotions. Among the questions are those related to competence, achievement, relationships with new colleagues, satisfaction, and enjoyment. Each professional new to student affairs encounters a range of problems and concerns about the future. The process of transition and change brings with it both doubt and anxiety.

In this chapter, the broad professional and personal issues influencing success in a first, crucial professional position will be discussed. False beliefs concerning work in student affairs and higher education will be identified. Finally, suggestions will be presented to assist new student affairs professionals to gain mastery of their new role.

A caveat is in order at this point. Not everything suggested in this chapter will be applicable to all new professionals. Readers must critically assess the ideas and suggestions presented and evaluate what has the most meaning for them. The institutional context, professional training, personal experience, and personal style of the professional will all influence the decisions that need to be made. The goal of this chapter is to discuss common concerns involved in a transition to a new role and to have readers begin the process of identifying concerns and developing strategies to confront their own set of issues.

PROFESSIONAL ISSUES

At a minimum, six professional issues must be addressed as a transition is made to a new position and to a professional role. These include: obtaining and using needed information, establishing expectations for performance, confronting the question of translating theory to practice, mapping the environment, establishing positive relationships with students, and continuing professional growth.

Obtaining and Using Information

As a new professional, a great deal of information will need to be mastered in a relatively short period of time. Some of that information will relate to the specific terms and conditions of employment, including employee benefits, retirement systems, insurance, educational benefits, and parking. Even though the content of the position is primary, do not ignore the need for good, solid information regarding conditions of employment. The decisions made in the first weeks on the job regarding insurance, retirement options, and other benefits will, at a minimum, influence the entire first year of employment. Take the time to read and understand all the information received. Do not be afraid to ask questions and get clarification, if necessary. For example, inadvertently parking in an inappropriate space could cause conflicts with potential colleagues, and not understanding expectations for participation in faculty/staff orientation activities could create a negative first impression.

A second, but equally critical base of information revolves around questions of how to get started in the new position. Some divisions of student affairs have established comprehensive orientation programs for new staff. If employed in an institution where such a program exists, take full advantage of such orientation (Baier, 1985). Usually such programs will cover the history and philosophy of the institution and the student affairs unit, critical policies and procedures, organizational responsibilities, and sources of help.

If, however, such a program does not exist, orientate yourself to the who, what, when, and where of the institution and the division. Initiative is required, but a great deal of information is available in most institutions to assist with that task. Read the catalog, course schedule, written policies and procedures, and old files. Ask colleagues about what is unclear. Seek out individuals who have been in the institution for some time and listen carefully to what they say. Study the organizational chart and learn the names of key players and actors in the institutional setting. Show interest in others and take the initiative in establishing relationships with them. Try to suspend judgment about the appropriateness of what is going on until a full and complete set of information is available on which to base a response.

Establishing Expectations

Administrative superiors and colleagues all have explicit and implicit expectations for performance. Stamatakos (1978) reminded new professionals to "Regularly ask yourself, 'Am I doing what my supervisor expects of me? What concrete or other evidence do I have that I am/am not satisfying my supervisor's expectations of me?' " (p. 325). Further, Stamatakos indicates that a job description is only a guide to what is expected. "The expectations of how a professional is to behave will have a great influence on how well the tasks defined can be accomplished" (Scher and Barr, 1979, p. 532). Clarity is essential and the new professional often must take the initiative to assure that their work performance meets expected standards. A number of expectations, however, are relatively easy to understand and can be applied in every professional setting. These include keeping your supervisor informed (Stamatakos, 1978); understanding the legal and organizational limits on your authority to act (Barr, 1988); meeting deadlines and following procedures (Pembroke, 1984); and producing accurate, thoughtful, well-planned work (Barr and Keating, 1985).

Other staff members also have expectations for the performance of a new colleague. Often these are even less readily discerned than those of a supervisor. Young (1985) indicated student affairs practitioners come into the field from a variety of academic backgrounds and experiences, and such differences may influence expectations. Ostroth (1981), however, indicates that most student affairs staff members are hired because of skills related to interpersonal communication, cooperation, and the ability to work with others.

Although great variation in background may exist among potential staff colleagues, the common skills delineated by Ostroth provide a new professional with a unique opportunity to learn from colleagues. A great deal can be learned from both observing and listening. Determine agency norms for office hours, attendance at events, dress, and demeanor through both observation and questioning. Listen carefully to both what is said and not said at staff meetings. Ask questions and elicit advice and assistance from your new staff colleagues. Often diametrically opposed points of view will surface regarding any specific person or issue. Judgments will also be required, although such judgments should not be made in haste. A decision to follow or reject institutional norms can only be made when institutional norms are known. Any decision will have consequences for the staff member's future within the organization (Scher and Barr, 1979, p. 531). Finally, request both positive and negative feedback and then attempt not to get defensive when the feedback is forthcoming. Peers and colleagues can provide a great deal of assistance in the process of achieving success in a new position.

Theory to Practice

Practitioners who emerge from a strong, theory-based program often experience dissonance between theory and actual practice in their first practitioner setting. Young (1985) indicated that this dissonance can even begin to emerge during practicum and internship experiences. What is learned in the classroom at times may not seem relevant or even valued in the new professional setting.

Stamatakos (1978) indicated that new professionals experience conflict because they know "what should or ought to be done and what is not being done" (p. 326). Often a major philosophical conflict arises for the new professional and frustration results. Some new professionals experience frustration with the theory-to-practice debate from an entirely different perspective. Usually this latter group includes individuals who come to student affairs from a different academic background. They become just as confused when they join an organization steeped in human development theory, and the organization uses that theory base to make decisions. Even conversations seem foreign to them as their colleagues discuss vectors, stages, and the like. Whether the frustration arises from a perceived difference between theory and practice, a perceived lack of knowledge on the part of new colleagues, or lack of a theory base on the part of the new professional, frustration will result.

The translation of human development or other theories to practice is difficult at best. The astute new professional proceeds very slowly and attempts to identify individuals who share beliefs or can help the new professional gain the skills and competencies needed to start on the translation process. If a new professional is in an environment where program efforts are either theoretical or merely based on tradition, there are positive steps which can be taken. Stamatakos (1978) suggested that a new professional (a) identify supporting elements; (b) identify obstacles; (c) assess the importance of those elements to the task; (d) determine the need for change; (e) develop a program proposal; and (f) present it in a positive, nonthreatening manner (p. 326). Knefelkamp and Wells (1983) cautioned that the use of theory really begins with practice and with asking pragmatic questions about the needs of students and effectiveness of professional practice. They further warned that "one cannot translate theory directly into practice. There is a critical middle step in the process: translating the theory into accurate characteristics of particular students in a particular environment" (Knefelkamp and Wells, 1983, p. 326).

The best advice to the new professional regarding this issue is to watch, observe, and assimilate prior to assuming that theory is not being used in your new environment. Once the needed data base is established, carefully develop a supporting framework to meet the goal of providing quality services for students.

Mapping the Environment

In addition to learning information about the institution, be able to apply that information in an effective manner. A new professional needs to get beyond the superficial and find out who really makes decisions and what the norms of behavior are within the institution.

Study the organizational chart and develop a private version identifying key assistants, secretaries, and others who provide access and information in the system (Barr and Keating, 1979). Observe others and ask questions with great frequency and precision.

To be successful in any position in higher education, horizons need to be extended beyond a specific job or agency. Actively work at understanding the "big picture." Stamatakos (1978) admonished young professionals, for example, to cultivate faculty. His advice is worth following, for not only are new friends and support systems developed, but understanding begins to emerge regarding the complexity of the institutional climate. Get involved in the life of the institution as well as the specific position or agency. Attend concerts, plays, lectures, and meetings. Such behavior will increase both knowledge and effectiveness as a student affairs administrator. With work, commitment, and dedication, a new professional will soon be able to differentiate between the crucial, the important, the necessary, and the irrelevant elements in the new environment.

Positive Relationships with Students

Most new professionals spend a great deal of their professional life working with students in both formal and informal settings. Thus, a critical element for professional success is establishing positive and productive working relationships with students. Often, this is easier said than done! Some new professionals over identify with students and do not clearly differentiate their professional role with students. Other new professionals fall into the trap of over identifying with their professional role and tend to structure their relationships with students in a rigid and authoritarian manner. Either extreme in behavior causes problems for both the new professional and for the students.

Monat (1985) indicated that he expects student affairs professionals "to speak up for students but never down to them" (p. 126). This is sound advice. Achieving a clear professional identity in your relationships with students is not an easy task, but one which must be mastered if professional success is to be achieved.

Some fairly simple guidelines seem to work best. First, identify someone on the campus who appears to have established positive working relationships with students and observe them. Second, identify both the written and unwritten rules of behavior on the campus and discuss them with both supervisors and your professional colleagues. Seek clarity on such questions as staff attendance and procedures. Third, define your role, the limitations in that role, and communicate that information to students. For example, as an advisor to a student organization, what are the limits of your authority? If an advisor can veto actions, students need to understand that the possibility exists for you to exercise your authority. Fourth, never promise students more than can be delivered. For instance, a promise of confidentiality may not be met under certain conditions. The ethical principles of your professional association will provide helpful guidance in this important area. Finally, be consistent, honest, and predictable in any relationships with students. Students are astute judges of people and can quickly sense insincerity. Students should reasonably expect that a professional be consistent and straightforward in a relationship.

Each new professional will need to develop their own personal style in relating to students. That style will be shaped, in part, by institutional practices, institutional rules, and the ethical codes of conduct governing professional practice.

Continued Professional Growth

One of the expectations an institution should have of all student affairs professionals is to "be intellectually and professionally active" (NASPA, 1988, p. 16). The methods of remaining active will vary from individual to individual. Active membership in a professional organization such as the National Association of Student Personnel Administrators (NASPA), the American College Personnel Association (ACPA), or one of the professional specialty groups such as the Association of College Unions International (ACUI) or the Association of College and University Housing Officers International (ACUHO-I) is a good first step. Journals and newsletters will provide information about current issues. Announcements of professional development opportunities on the state, regional, and national levels will also be available and may be of value.

One relatively easy way to assure professional growth is to keep up-to-date on issues and new practices in student affairs through professional reading. Journals, books, and newsletters are all sources of ideas and information that can be put to use in your professional practice. Keeping up-to-date on current issues in higher education through regular perusal of *The Chronicle of Higher Education* is equally important. Current knowledge assists in making positive contributions as the institution faces new challenges in the years ahead.

Invest both time and personal money, if necessary, in your future as a student affairs professional. Attend workshops and conferences. New material will be learned and connections with other professional colleagues will be developed. Take the risk of submitting a program idea and making a presentation at a conference. Testing ideas with colleagues is a certain way to assure continued professional growth.

Local staff development programs also provide a viable option for continued professional growth. Whether such opportunities are offered on institutional, divisional, or departmental level, take the initiative to get involved and participate in such programs. At the very least, an extended network of persons on campus interested in similar issues will be established. More than likely, however, new knowledge will be gained or skills and competencies developed.

Finally, consider resuming a formal educational degree program. The structured institutional learning experiences can help a new professional remain intellectually active and professionally aware.

However, the decision to pursue advanced studies (e.g., doctoral degree, special certification) may crucially affect a professional's career and educational advancement. Some significant considerations are financial (e.g., tuition and lack of a regular paycheck), disruption of continuous full-time work, family concerns, and the timing related to gaining practical experience and professional growth in one's career.

FALSE BELIEFS

There are a number of false beliefs that can influence our effectiveness as student affairs professionals. Some of these false beliefs center around the political nature of the higher education enterprise.

The first is a deeply held belief that worthwhile concepts should and will be supported. Barr and Keating (1979) cautioned that, in addition to a concept being worthwhile, concept criteria must be cost effective, consistent, and in line with institutional priorities.

Second, some believe that opposition to ideas and concepts is due to bad intentions on the part of the other party (Barr and Keating, 1979). This is not necessarily true. Sometimes individuals see the world from a different perspective and have different information than those proposing the idea. Before bad intentions are assumed, try to understand the source of the opposition. The concern expressed by others may indeed be legitimate.

Third, some feel that outside pressure should have no influence on professional practice, but both internal and external forces have a real and very direct influence on higher education institutions and student affairs (Barr, 1985). For example, drug abuse is of national concern and cannot be ignored by colleges and universities. National political issues such as the threat of war have long influenced higher education institutions. Changes in the law and interpretation of the law will affect both policies and procedures. No institution or student affairs agency is immune to outside influences, and astute professionals learn to effectively deal with such pressures when they occur.

Fourth, many student affairs professionals feel they should and can understand the pressures faced by their administrative superior (Barr and Keating, 1979). As higher education becomes more complex, many administrators are dealing with new pressures. Expectations of resource management and planning are examples. Sometimes it is impossible to understand all the pressures, and it is not necessary to do so.

Fifth, there is a temptation to believe that details are not important. While it is necessary to understand the larger implications of professional practice, the astute new staff member recognizes that the big picture is filled with details. Successful programs and interventions only occur when all the details are taken care of in a timely and efficient manner. Mastery of planning and program implementation skills requires attention to detail.

Sixth, many believe a negative decision is forever (Barr and Keating, 1979). Several factors influence decisions, including key actors in the process, the current context, timing, and political currents flowing on and off the campus. The astute professional attempts to determine the reasons for a negative decision and then strives to modify their proposal, resubmitting the idea when all factors are more positive.

Other false beliefs which can influence professional practice probably exist. The important point is that new professionals should be cautious about making assumptions about people, systems, or institutions before gathering all the facts.

SUGGESTIONS FOR PRACTICE

Several concrete steps are available to new professionals to maximize their success in a new position.

Seek a mentoring relationship. Young (1985), Barr and Keating (1979), and others asserted that a positive mentoring relationship has great potential. Identifying such potential mentors is not an easy task and a relationship must be developed through mutual trust and loyalty. One person may not be able to provide the full range of guidance that is needed and may not be directly available on campus. In fact, some individuals, both on and off campus, may be able to provide support and direction in specific areas. Such relationships must never be one-sided. A person seeking help can also provide valuable information and perspective to a mentor. Seasoned professionals can help new professionals learn and grow, and intentionality is needed for developing and nurturing such growth producing professional relationships.

Develop new interests. Balance is needed between personal and professional lives. Expanded interests help to maintain perspective, provide stimulation, and give a needed respite from the pressures of work. Scher and Barr (1979) suggested trying something you have always wanted to do, whether it is mastery of a skill or studying a subject. Outside involvement helps an individual gain and keep a perspective on the professional task.

Take care of yourself. The popular press is filled with descriptions of workaholics. Becoming a workaholic is easy in student affairs because hours are erratic and the work is interesting. Therefore developing personal support networks is critical and should be a priority (Barr and Keating, 1979). In addition, personal, physical, and mental health concerns cannot be ignored.

Maintain friendships. One of the inevitable costs of moving to a new position is separation from friends and relatives. Work at keeping those relationships alive and active through letters and phone calls. During the process of change, support is needed and will not occur without intentional effort.

Maintain a sense of humor. A good, healthy sense of humor helps many through difficult times. Research also indicates that happier people feel less stress and work more effectively with others. Work should be enjoyable and a sense of humor helps maintain that enjoyment.

Be true to yourself. Stamatakos (1978) and Scher and Barr (1979) admonished new professionals to be true to themselves as they go about their work. The advice of the Hebrew sage Hillel is particularly relevant, "If I am not for myself, who is for me?" (Goldin, 1962). "Self-worth as a professional and as a person is closely related to the honesty and enthusiasm we manifest in the practice of our profession" (Stamatakos, 1979,

p. 330). Each professional will need to determine if the current environment meets essential needs and supports important values. If not, then a decision to leave must be made in a professional and responsible manner.

SUMMARY

The transition to a new professional position in student affairs is filled with excitement, challenge, and change. Inevitably, problems and frustrations will emerge. Success will come to those who exercise their skills and are patient as they encounter new people, problems, opportunities, and challenges. The key to success lies in the ability of the new professional to assume a new role in a positive, straightforward manner and to be slow in making assumptions about people, programs, and policies.

REFERENCES

Baier, J. (1985). Recruiting and training competent staff. In M.J. Barr and L.A. Keating (Eds.), *Developing effective student services programs* (pp. 212-33). San Francisco: Jossey-Bass Publishers.

Barr, M.J. (1985). Internal and external forces influencing programming. In M.J. Barr and L.A. Keating (Eds.), *Developing effective student services programs* (pp. 62-82). San Francisco: Jossey-Bass Publishers.

Barr, M.J. (1988). *Student services and the law: A guide for practitioners.* San Francisco: Jossey-Bass Publishers.

Barr, M.J., and Keating, L.A. (1979). No program is an island. In M.J. Barr and L.A. Keating (Eds.), *New directions for student services: Establishing effective student services programs* (p. 7). San Francisco: Jossey-Bass Publishers.

Barr, M.J., and Keating, L.A. (Eds.). (1985). *Developing effective student services programs.* San Francisco: Jossey-Bass Publishers.

Goldin, G. (Ed.). (1962). *Ethics of the fathers.* New York: Hebrew Publishing Company.

Knefelkamp, L., and Wells, E. (1983). Translating student development theory into practice for student affairs personnel. Unpublished manuscript.

Monat, W. (1985). Role of student services: A presidential perspective. In M.J. Barr and L.A. Keating (Eds.), *Developing effective student services programs* (p. 126). San Francisco: Jossey-Bass Publishers.

National Association of Student Personnel Administrators. (1988). *A perspective on student affairs.* Washington, D.C.: Author.

Ostroth, D. (1981). Competencies for entry level professionals: What do employers look for when hiring new staff? *Journal of College Student Personnel,* 22, 5-11.

Pembroke, W.J. (1985). Fiscal restraints on program development. In M.J. Barr and L.A. Keating (Eds.), *Developing effective student services programs* (pp. 83-109). San Francisco: Jossey-Bass Publishers.

Scher, M.A., and Barr, M.J. (1979). Beyond graduate school: Strategies for survival. *Journal of College Student Personnel,* 19, 325-30.

Stamatakos, L.C. (1978). Unsolicited advice for new professionals. *Journal of College Student Personnel,* 19, 325-30.

Young, R.D. (1985). Impressions of the development of professional identity: From programs to practice. *NASPA Journal,* 23(2), 50-60.

Chapter 3

Using Theory and Performing Research in Everyday Practice

Roger B. Winston, Jr.

Following is a typical page from the diary of a new professional for a Tuesday during the fall semester.

November 15

8:15 a.m.   Arrive at office; greeted by secretary with following messages:

(1) Your boss wants to see you at 11:15 a.m. (this time conflicts with previously made appointment with a student who is having adjustment problems)

(2) Campus police report investigating an attack on a student which occurred in the parking lot at 3:15 a.m.

(3) Building supervisor reports that three custodians failed to report to work

(4) Meeting with parent of student who seems to be having severe emotional problems has been scheduled for 10:45 a.m.

(5) Building supervisor reports that third floor lounge has been "trashed" for the third consecutive day

Using Theory and Performing Research in Everyday Practice 31

	(6) Chairman of the film series reports that the movie scheduled for this evening has not yet arrived.
	(7) Monthly report is due today, rather than tomorrow, to accommodate your boss' trip out of town
	(8) Secretary needs to be off this afternoon for a physician's appointment (there's no one to cover the office between 2:00 and 4:00 p.m.)
	(9) Coteacher of paraprofessional training course is ill, and will not be able to teach class at 4:30 today (you are unprepared to cover the material)
	(10) New friend (with whom you are developing a romantic relationship) called to confirm dinner at 6:30 p.m.
9:05 a.m.	Physical plant calls to indicate that the power will be off in the building at 10:00 a.m. to 1:00 p.m. (request secretary to begin making calls to others in the building to inform them of power outage)
9:10 a.m.	Student comes in to complain about unfair treatment by paraprofessional (she is very emotional)
9:50 a.m.	Chairman of campus committee calls to remind you that it is important for you to attend 2:00 p.m. meeting
10:20 a.m.	College president's secretary calls to ask where the president is to speak tonight (you didn't know she had been invited)
10:30 a.m.	Parent calls from airport to indicate that he will be late for the 10:45 a.m. meeting
10:33 a.m.	Call boss to reschedule meeting, explaining about parent (boss is irritated, but reschedules meeting for 1:00 p.m.)
10:35 a.m.	Begin trying to locate student leaders to find out who invited the president to speak tonight and

	what the plans are for the event (unable to reach anyone)
11:40 a.m.	Parent arrives for conference (he is upset about his daughter; hints that he thinks the college is not "looking after her properly," and said he is going to talk to his friend on the Board of Trustees)
12:20 p.m.	Parent leaves conference dissatisfied
12:30 p.m.	Eat burger at Greasy Spoon across the street from office
1:00 p.m.	Meet with boss (he wants a survey of needed repairs to lounges by 5:00 today; he is not pleased when told you cannot get your monthly report in today; he does not know anything about the president speaking tonight and is concerned that you do not either; you are instructed to make the president's appearance your first priority).
1:45 p.m.	Arrive at office to discover it locked with a note from secretary stating that she has gone to doctor's appointment (two unhappy students are waiting outside the locked door)
1:55 p.m.	Find student worker to keep office open and answer the telephone (request student worker to try to find out who is involved with inviting the president to speak)
2:10 p.m.	Depart for committee meeting
2:20 p.m.	Arrive late to committee meeting to discover that a quorum was not present and that it has been rescheduled for next week
2:35 p.m.	Arrive at your office to find president of student organization that invited the president to speak waiting (she does not know what arrangements have been made; she cannot find the program chairman who was supposed to have made all the arrangements; no room has been scheduled for meeting)

2:50 p.m.	Call building supervisor to instruct him to set a meeting in room 322 for president's talk; call president's office to tell where she is to speak; get the student organization president to begin contacting people to make sure there is a "presentable" audience for the president's talk
3:45 p.m.	Secretary calls to say that she will be unable to return to work this afternoon.
4:00 p.m.	Go to library and read material quickly to be covered in paraprofessional class
4:30 p.m.	Teach class (students know you were unprepared; class doesn't go well)
6:00 p.m.	Call student organization president to check on program (informed that it looks like attendance will be light)
6:15 p.m.	Call friend to say that you cannot get away for dinner
6:20 p.m.	Begin calling students to attempt to encourage attendance at president's program
6:45 p.m.	Arrive at room where president is to speak and find that it is not properly arranged (you and several students rearrange chairs)
7:00 p.m.	President arrives to meet students (only 12 students are present)
8:30 p.m.	President departs (not in very good mood because of small turnout)
8:45 p.m.	Eat a pizza in Greasy Spoon (get a good case of heartburn)
10:00 p.m.	Arrive at apartment and call friend (friend is unhappy about the late cancellation of the dinner date and seems suspicious about your explanation)
11:30 p.m.	Go to bed (set alarm for 6:00 a.m. because there is a student leaders' breakfast at 7:30 a.m. on campus)

To say this diary entry is a full day is an understatement. The day, however, is often typical of the demands made on new professionals early in their careers. New professionals need to pay careful attention to administrative and organizational details and to assure that routine and often mundane tasks are performed. Accordingly, many new professionals sneer when older professionals and preparation program faculty members urge them to employ theory and research findings in their everyday work. New professionals argue, "Where is there time?" and besides, "What theory explains what I do on a daily basis?"

This chapter examines the issues that directly address the important question, "Is student affairs a professional field?" The chapter also puts into perspective the use of theory in everyday practice and offers suggestions about how research findings can (and should) relate to the practice of college student affairs.

THE RELATIONSHIPS OF THEORY TO PRACTICE

Schon (1987, p. 4) asked the pivotal question for student affairs, "Can student affairs professionals take the high ground (where problems lend themselves to solution through the application of research-based theory) overlooking the swamp (where the problems are messy, intertwined in obscure institutional politics, overinflated egos, and students who are attending college for a plethora of reasons?"—ranging from a last chance for a party before entering the adult world, to finding an "appropriate mate"). In fact, Schon asserted that practitioners are not often faced with "well-formed structures . . .," but are instead faced with "indeterminate situations" (p. 4). Most knowledgeable people know that student affairs began and usually finds itself in the swamp of indeterminate situations. After all, the first deans of men and women came into being because faculty members no longer wanted to deal with the messy problems of students' personal lives outside the classroom. In addition, many college presidents today assert that, to an institution, the true value of student affairs is working in the swamp of students' untidy issues, concerns, and problems. The issues, concerns, and problems are often expressed with an overabundance of youthful exuberance and impetuosity, and in areas where others in the institution fear to tread.

As Rodgers (1983) and Carpenter, Miller, and Winston (1980) pointed out, however, too often practitioners are heard to argue that student affairs is not, and should not be thought of as, a profession. Student affairs is instead a common sense field of endeavor that is only needlessly complicated by the introduction of ideas about theory and research-based practice. The common sense school of practice contends that student affairs practitioners' responsibilities center on assuring the smooth functioning of the institution and providing services that are designed to address students' problems after they are encountered. There is no central educational mission for student affairs commensurate with that of the faculty in the traditional academic disciplines. As a consequence, there is little need for sophisticated theories of student development or organizational functioning because they are pretentious and just get in the way.

There are several guiding principles for those who advocate a professional perspective of student affairs, in opposition to the common sense school. A professional might be defined as a person who, because of education and experience has command of a constellation of theories that describes, and sometimes predicts, human behavior and the ways that groups and organizations develop and function. The professional also possesses skills that can promote change in individuals and organizations. The professional practitioner adheres to a code of ethical conduct, is committed to the ideal of service to humanity, and contributes to the profession through active involvement in professional organizations. The professional is dedicated to creating environments within higher education institutions for students that contribute to the

- education of their intellects
- development of healthy, fully functioning personalities
- promotion of democratic ideals and fundamental justice
- development of wholesome lifestyles

- adoption of a set of considered moral, ethical, and/or religious values

Advocates of student affairs as a theory-based profession, however, have several difficult theoretical problems that must be squarely addressed. First, a view of theory, as usually conceptualized in the physical sciences, inhibits its application to student affairs. Second, there is often confusion about the differences between basic philosophical assumptions, scientific theories, and process models. Third, many practitioners do not have sophisticated understandings of contemporary theories and are thus unable to apply them.

Theory in Student Affairs Practice

Argyris and Schon (1978) argued that theories in the social and behavioral sciences can have three different functions: explanation, prediction, and control.

Theories may be explanatory by setting forth propositions from which events can be explained. For example, the generally mild depression and self-doubt often evident in college freshmen during the first few days or weeks on campus can be explained by what is popularly called "homesickness," or a lack of a sense of competence. The freshman also experiences undeveloped senses of emotional and instrumental autonomy.

A predictive theory sets forth propositions from which inferences about future events may be made. Based on a knowledge of a given group of students' levels of emotional and instrumental autonomy, basic personality characteristics, and the nature or quality of the interpersonal environment in the residence hall, one could predict the level of homesickness likely to be experienced by students as a group.

Theory used for purposes of control describes the conditions under which events of a certain kind may be made to occur. By establishing an environment that has high stimulation and support; enjoyable activities; and a resident assistant who greets new arrivals, spends time getting to know them, initiates processes to help roommates to become acquainted, and who communicates a willingness to be helpful, one can use theory to control the duration and intensity of homesickness experienced by new students as a group during the first weeks on campus.

Control refers to conditions that can be established in the environment that will increase the probability of certain behaviors occurring while inhibiting others. The individual student, however, still has the power to determine how to respond to the environment and can resist the environmental press. A student encountering an environment that is not compatible with their needs or wishes, can adapt to the prevailing press, flee the environmentally induced stress, psychologically withdraw by insulating themselves from the surroundings, or attempt to modify the environment to satisfy their needs or wants.

The paradigm shift, a contrary point of view (Caple, 1987a, 1987b; Kuh, Whitt, and Shedd, 1987), argued that the principal problems with understanding and using theory in the profession is that theory views the world from a traditional scientific perspective that views phenomena from a mechanical cause-and-effect perspective. Advocates of this new, radical phenomenology argue that the basic assumptions about the nature of science/theory are not adequate, or even appropriate, to describe the phenomena college students and higher education organizations with which student affairs practitioners work.

Kuh, Whitt, and Shedd (1987) maintained that an adequate theory must view student affairs practice as

- *perspectival:* seen from the viewer's experience, values, and expectations only, rather than as objective which maintains that events can be studied from an outside, value-neutral perspective
- *complex and diverse:* there are multiple realities, not a common shared experience, such that the whole is greater than the sum of its parts, rather than reductionistic which maintains that events can be explained and predicted by reducing them to their simplest components
- *heterarchic:* order in a system is created by networks of mutual influence and constraints rather than hierarchic which maintains that systems are ordered vertically with authority and responsibility flowing from the top down

- *holonomic:* "events are dynamic processes of interaction and differentiation in which information about the whole is present in each of the parts" (p. 14) rather than mechanical where actions are predictable and events can be described as sequential
- *indeterminate:* future events are unpredictable and that ambiguity and disorder are the norm rather than determinate where events operate in predictable and rational ways that can be influenced by rational means such as planning and goal setting
- *mutual shaping:* "events are generated by complex reciprocal processes that blur distinctions between cause and effect" (p. 14) rather than linear causality which holds that events have finite and identifiable causes
- *morphogenetic:* change is evolutionary and spontaneous thereby producing unanticipated outcomes rather than assembled which maintains that change can result from purposeful action that will consistently produce a predicted outcome.

Kuh, Whitt, and Shedd's view clearly indicates some of the major deficiencies of current theories of student development such as Chickering's (1969) psychosocial, Perry's (1970) intellectual, or Kohlberg's (1969) moral development theory—all of which rest on rather traditional scientific assumption structures and are primarily descriptive (they attempt to explain behavior as it has been observed). The theories' major shortcomings are a lack of universal principles that specify the necessary and sufficient conditions for bringing about movement from one stage to a more complex stage (or stimulating accomplishment of a developmental task), while also taking into account what is already known about individual differences and the influences of various environmental factors. Specifically, the profession lacks theories that are detailed enough to serve the control function with efficiency and consistency (Argyris and Schon, 1978).

Student Development Theories as Bases for Practice

Criticisms of student development theories as bases for practice rest on a fundamental misunderstanding of the nature of theory. Theory is an abstraction from reality! As a consequence, one seldom sees a "walking theory" in a student. Therefore, most student development theories are intended to describe the behavior of students as a class of persons; there will always be individual exceptions as long as students have freedom of choice and volition. Theories, although often not stated as such, are really communicating that certain types of students from specific backgrounds, placed in a particular academic environment, will tend to behave in predictable ways. Theories of student development, whether psychosocial, career, moral or intellectual, are scientific and are a matter of levels of probability or conditional certainty. The level of certainty in the behavioral sciences will always be lower than that found in most physical sciences. Describing students' development of autonomy or intimate relationships, for example, will never possess a similar degree of certainty as propositions in mathematics such as $4+4=8$.

Knefelkamp (1984) noted that student development theories are contextual in that they were developed from the study of specific populations in a limited and often imprecisely described range of environments. These limitations must be recognized, and careful attention must be directed at identifying how those limitations may affect the translation of the theory to the population of students with whom the practitioner desires to apply the theory.

To argue, as the paradigm shift does, that traditional theories about human behavior are not applicable because they are incomplete or lack mathematical precision, seems quite myopic. The current reexamination of theories is healthy; however, the reexamination is not convincing as an argument to abandon the scientific method or to discount years of careful observation and research. Rather, the aforementioned phenomenology should serve to remind practitioners of the need to collect data systematically about their particular student clientele, study the unique features of the institution's environment carefully and periodically, and experimentally evaluate the application of developmental theories to their institutions and students through careful planning and sound evaluation techniques.

Assumptions, Theories, and Process Models

Blocher (1987) pointed out, concerning theories of counseling which apply as well to student affairs practice in general, that practitioners need to differentiate among philosophical assumptions, theories, and process models.

Philosophical Assumptions

Philosophical assumptions, by definition, are empirically untestable and are usually abstractions drawn from basic values and beliefs about the human experience. Kuh, Whitt, and Shedd (1987, p. 35) contended that, "The expectation that student affairs staff can and should take decisive action to influence specific aspects of students' development is a relatively recent addition to the responsibilities typically assumed by student affairs" and was not explicitly stipulated as a mission for the field in the *Student Personnel Point of View* (1937, 1949) statements. Associated with these "new" missions were the concepts of proaction and intentional intervention. Kuh and his colleagues have identified some very basic changes in the underlying assumptions about student affairs' mission. Regrettably, these assumptions have been presented as applications of developmental theory rather than as fundamental statements about the purposes of practice. For the first time, student affairs practitioners asserted their educational responsibility commensurate with that of traditional academic instruction rather than as a purely supportive service function for academic learning or a means for controlling students' behavior and maintaining public order and private morality.

The emergence of a new sense of mission began to gain widespread acceptance just as theories about students' development were gaining extensive recognition. These theories opened new possibilities for the field, but they did not mandate a change in its mission. No theory, regardless of how well formulated and empirically tested, can be used to justify the proposition that student affairs' mission should include "intentional intervention." The profession, however, seems to have stopped short of clearly answering for itself, or for the general academic community, the fundamental question, "Development for what?" Development is a process, not a product. Practitioners need to identify more precisely the goals of proaction and intentional intervention. What should students learn? How will students be different as a direct result of a given student affairs intervention, as opposed to nonintervention? Purposeful developmental interventions are not value free.

Theories

"Theories focus on and guide empirical inquiry and define the rules of evidence" (Blocher, 1987, p. 68). Theories of student development are adequate to the extent that they explain or accurately predict students' behavior under specified environmental conditions and emotional states. These theories, however, must be specific enough so that some kinds of behavior can prove their propositions false. The adherents of the new paradigm argue that all current student development theories fail to recognize the importance that chance or unpredictable events play in influencing an individual's course of development, and, because the paths of development can be chaotic and unpredictable (i.e., second-order change), it is not possible to formulate a scientific theory of individual development that is composed of causally related steps, stages, processes, or positions.

The advocates of the new paradigm, however, offer little to replace developmental theory as guides or aids to understanding students' development. As Drum and Lawler (1988, p. 26) noted, "though imperfect, conflicting, and incomplete, . . . [human development theories] remain the best guidelines we have in our journey toward fuller understanding of the marvelously complex maturation process of the . . . self." Apparently, the new paradigm advocates would have student affairs practitioners return to the common sense, do-what-seems-right approach to practice that was evident during the early days of the profession. If human behavior is completely unpredictable and, therefore, cannot be influenced in any anticipated ways, then student affairs practitioners can only react to events. Without any reliable tools or methodologies available to manage or impact what happens, professional practice becomes a matter of random trial-and-error reactions.

Process Models

Practitioners can use theories of student development to create interventions that are designed to influence particular areas of students' lives. Blocher (1987) suggested that process models are cognitive maps that guide practitioners' action. Process models are applications of theory but are not themselves theories.

Many valuable process or program/intervention planning models have been proposed that are based on varying degrees of theoretical sophistication and expansiveness. Some of the models making explicit use of theories of college student development include the Tomorrow's Higher Education (THE) model (Miller and Prince, 1976), cube model (Morrill, Hurst, and Oetting, 1980; Hurst and Jacobson, 1985), grounded formal theory model (Rodgers and Widick, 1980; Rodgers, 1983); practice-to-theory-to-practice model (Knefelkamp, 1984); intentionally structured group model (Winston, Bonney, Miller, and Dagley, 1988); and the developmental interventions model (Drum and Lawler, 1988).

Developmental theories play crucial roles in these process models because they provide the practitioner a framework for planning, implementing, and evaluating interventions. Process models are operationalized theories and serve as road maps that help practitioners determine when or whether they have arrived at their desired destination.

Understanding and Using Theory

Rodgers (1983) asserted that there is a four-location continuum of understanding theories. At Location One, the person has an amorphous, vague understanding (persons at this position have been introduced to major concepts and have some familiarity with the terminology unique to that theory). Persons at Location Two are able to define terms within the theory's context and to describe the basic operating principles that govern the system. At Location Three, persons have a much better understanding of the theory than in the previous locations; they have an operational understanding which allows them to comprehend the theory's logic and to extrapolate relatively accurately beyond the authors' specific findings. "Concepts . . . [have] taken on shape, structure, and meaning" (p. 115). Finally, at Location Four persons have "intimate familiarity with the constructs and subconstructs of the theory, knowledge of how developmental change takes place in terms of the constructs of the theory, and an intimate familiarity with the means of measuring the constructs and the advantages and limitations of each" (p. 115). It is only at Location Four that practitioners can truly use developmental theory to design effective programs and interventions. As several studies have documented, this level of understanding is still quite rare in the field (Heineman and Strange, 1984; Strange, 1981, 1983).

The level of understanding is directly related to the differences between practitioners' espoused theories and their theories in use (Argyris and Schon, 1978; Argyris, Putnam, and Smith, 1987; Schon, 1987). Espoused theories of action are what one gets from "educated" practitioners when they are asked to describe what they would do under a certain set of circumstances. Theories in use, on the other hand, are the basic assumptions, principles, and values practitioners actually use as they go about their work. Theories in use include assumptions about self, others, and the situation, and the connections among action, consequence, and situation.

Often there are incongruencies between espoused theories and theories in use; or to put it in colloquial language, there is a gap between what we say and what we do. Many student affairs practitioners espouse student development, often including the term in their position titles, while operating in daily practice in an atheoretical, sometimes unreflective common sense manner. This common sense manner is explained in part because the practitioners' level of understanding of student development theories is usually at Locations One or Two. The practitioners do not have a sufficiently sophisticated understanding of student development theories for them to become an integral part of their theories in use. Practitioners, therefore, espouse student development principles but continue to do what must be done to keep the institution running (which often involves attending to mundane details, processing reams of forms, and performing seemingly endless routine humdrum tasks). In reality, there is very little connection between the two.

One observation is that many practitioners, when describing a practice or policy as developmental actually mean, "This is the most convenient or less troublesome way to do it." The misuse of the term student development has produced much of the underserved and misguided criticism of developmental theory. Miller, Winston, and Mendenhall (1983, pp. 21-22) observed, "In some instances the term 'student development' has been used to replace 'student affairs' . . . in position titles. In many cases the name change has been cosmetic at best and has not influenced in any significant way either organizational structures or daily contact with students."

RESEARCH THAT INFORMS PRACTICE

Research in the social and behavioral sciences is always a matter of compromise. Considering that people are the subject matter of this research, there are ethical limits that restrict how rigidly conditions can be controlled or manipulated and how pure interventions can be. All major codes of professional ethics in the human sciences require researchers to place the welfare of human participants as the paramount consideration when designing and conducting studies. As a consequence, the degree of control and measurement precision common in the physical sciences is not possible when conducting research with humans. Thorngate (1976) asserted the principle of commensurate complexity, which holds that it is impossible for a theory of social behavior to be simultaneously general, accurate, and simple. For example, the more accurately a theory describes behavior the more likely the theory will be complex; or the more general a simple theory, the less likely it can accurately predict specific behaviors. This principle also applies to research methodologies; all social behavior methodologies make compromises among these three aspects.

Weick (1979) expanded on Thorngate's principle and suggested that these three aspects can be visualized on the face of a clock, with general at 12:00, accurate at 4:00, and simple at 8:00 (see Figure 1). In an attempt to maximize any two aspects or virtues, the researcher must sacrifice the third one. Within this context, traditional quantitative research methodologies usually fall somewhere between 12:00 and 4:00, say at 2:00. The 2:00 approach attempts to formulate an explanation of phenomena as accurately as possible. Objectivity, large-scale data collections, unbiased sampling techniques, and statistical estimations of error are tools for assuring as high a level of accuracy and as a wide applicability as possible. In pursuit of broad applicability (traditionally known as high external validity) and precision of prediction (traditionally known as high internal validity), the resulting product is often so complicated that it has limited utility for directing professional practice. The epitome of this approach is laboratory experimentation. Laboratory experimentation allows for relatively tight control and precision of measurement of variables, but the artificiality of the setting limits its application in the daily work with students.

Research that concentrates on accuracy and simplicity is most closely associated with qualitative methodologies or naturalistic inquiry techniques. Qualitative methods favor data collected by indepth interviews, case studies, observation, and analysis of existing documents and records such as disciplinary files, admission applications, and budgets. Qualitative methodology is favored by the adherents of the new paradigm. They assert that in data collection "only the human instrument can use intuition and tacit knowledge as well as reason and logic in collecting and

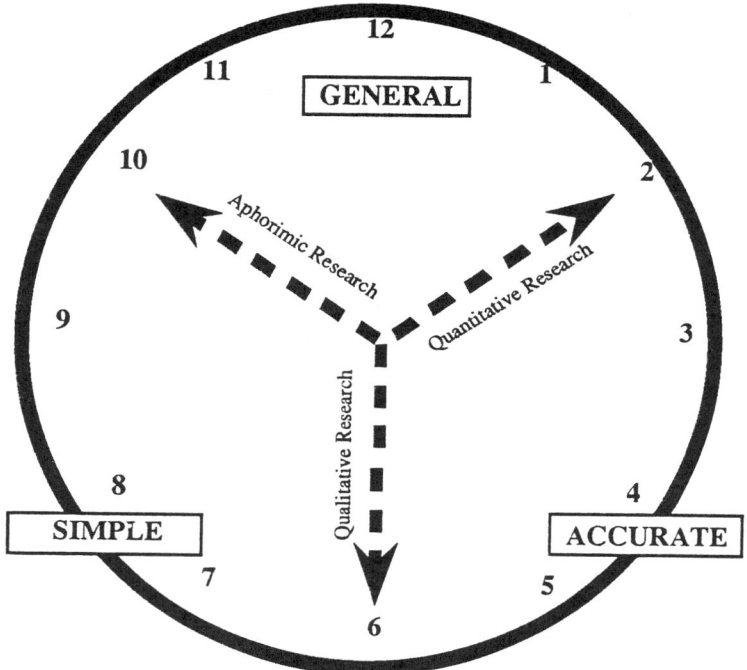

Figure 1: Weick's Taxonomy of Research Methodologies
Based on a figure from Weick (1979, p. 36). Reproduced from *The Social Psychology of Organizing* (2nd ed.) by permission of Addison-Wesley Publishing Company, Reading, MA.

analyzing information. And only the human instrument can accumulate understanding with sensitivity to context, to the perceptual world of respondents, and to the investigator's own beliefs, values, and assumptions" (Kuh, Shedd, and Whitt, 1987, p. 82).

Quantitative (2:00) research does not effectively address the simplicity criterion and qualitative (6:00) research methods sacrifice generalizability. Because these methodologies do not attempt to select research participants to be representative of a larger group (population), the findings must be interpreted cautiously, always being aware that the conclusions are subject to distortions due to the idiosyncrasies of the small number of individuals studied.

Weick (1979) argued that there is a third kind of research that he calls creation of aphorisms, which fits at 10:00 on his clock face of research methodologies. Aphorisms express the researcher's private understandings of events or situations which are distilled, rather than deduced, from experience. These kinds of knowledge are general and simple, which makes them especially valuable because they are "simple, easy to remember, portable, and seem to apply in a wide variety of situations" but have modest accuracy, i.e., they are difficult to apply in concrete situations (Weick, 1979, p. 39). The principal value of aphorisms is that they can help practitioners see facets of problems in new ways, ask new questions, and honestly face the state of the current certainty, or uncertainty, about the phenomenon.

All three kinds of research strategies can contribute to understanding college students, their environments, and higher education as complex organizations. Qualitative research methodologies are valuable because they can assist practitioners in understanding college students' personal experiences. Through careful, systematic observations and indepth interviews, practitioners can see the effects of attempts to assist students gain the maximum benefits possible from the college experience. Insights are gained beyond those possible through questionnaires and other paper-and-pencil data collection techniques, no matter how sophisticated. Naturalistic inquiries are most likely to inform practitioners about how students perceive their efforts and can often stimulate development of new and innovative interventions or policies. Naturalistic inquiries also have the advantage of requiring student affairs professionals to critically examine the applicability of existing theories of college student development to the student population present in the institution in which the practitioner works.

As a research tool, however, naturalistic inquiry should also generate general hypotheses that can be tested through traditional quantitative techniques. Quantitative methods can serve a validation function for the theories that each practitioner should formulate individually, whether general or specific, about students' behavior.

Aphorisms can serve to transmit the values of the profession and to communicate to new professionals the understandings about students as developing human beings and the truths about higher education organizations and their unique culture. The simplicity of aphorisms make them ideal for acculturating new professionals into the field and give novices starting points for their practice as professionals, which must also include some attention to research with the constituent population.

NEW PROFESSIONALS' USE OF THEORY AND RESEARCH

Consider the example of a new professional's day presented at the beginning of the chapter. How can the new professional use theory and research to deal with the problems presented there? The first thing that must be acknowledged is that much of what new professionals do has little to do with being a professional. Many higher education institutions are guilty of misusing student affairs professionals by failing to provide them with adequate support staff, equipment, and facilities. A suggested approach is that new professionals analyze what they do each day and classify their activities into four broad categories:

- organizational maintenance functions
- staff supervision and training functions
- educational functions
- contribution to knowledge

Organizational maintenance functions are those activities that must be performed to keep the organization ambulatory, which often includes attention to details and performance of many mundane tasks. (One wag defined academic administration as a series of meaningless tasks that have no consequences unless they are not performed.) Examples of organizational maintenance functions are assuring that equipment is available, facilities are properly cleaned and maintained, institutional procedures and policies are followed, and appropriate forms are completed and properly filed. These activities are crucial to the successful functioning of new professionals because failure to attend to such details may cause both students and supervisors to question the new professionals' basic competence and will usually undermine their other efforts.

Performing many organizational maintenance tasks does not usually require a graduate degree, high levels of intellect, or broad knowledge. Consequently, common sense and life experience are most valuable in the organizational maintenance function area. Professional skills are needed, however, to create means for addressing administrative and maintenance details that leave sufficient time to attend to other tasks that require sophisticated understanding and skills. In most settings, new professionals could easily occupy 10 or 12 hours per day with these matters (if they allow themselves to do so). New professionals who do not develop means for accomplishing these tasks efficiently often fail to advance in the field. Personal management skills such as time management, delegation of responsibility, and goal setting are essential for success.

Staff supervision and training functions generally require more of the practitioner's professional knowledge and skills. Understanding theories about human behavior and how to influence that behavior in positive, productive ways require practitioners to use their graduate educations in areas such as communications skills, helping strategies, and personnel evaluations techniques. Success is dependent on a combination of personality characteristics (of the professional and the staff with whom they work) and knowledge and skill in leadership and motivation.

In this area, new professionals are encouraged to use a relatively simple process in deciding on appropriate strategies:

Step 1: analyze the situation and identify desired outcomes
Step 2: specify the principal forces, conditions, and other factors (such as personal idiosyncrasies) that are operating in the situation

Step 3: evaluate alternative strategies in terms of probability of producing desired outcomes
Step 4: select the most promising alternative(s)
Step 5: predict outcomes based on theories of human and/or organizational behavior theories
Step 6: act
Step 7: evaluate whether desired outcomes were produced and how well the theory performed its prediction function.

Most practitioners often fail to initiate Steps 5 and 7.

Frequently, writing out the predictions based on the theory and explicitly stating what evidence can disprove the theory is helpful. Proving or disproving the theory means collecting data that will be useful in determining how well the theory performed. In so doing, practitioners can begin to select theories that seem to work with their unique student populations. As a result, new professionals will focus on making careful observations and performing meticulous analyses early in their careers. To be successful, new professionals need to be reflective practitioners. The practitioner should keep in mind, however, that "professional practice, applied science, and research-based technique occupy a critically important though limited territory, bounded on several sides by artistry. There is an art of problem framing, an art of implementation, and an art of improvisation—all necessary to mediate the use in practice of applied science [theory] and technique" (Schon, 1987, p. 13).

In the third area (educational functions), new professionals are called upon to apply their knowledge of human development and learning by implementing strategies for influencing the content and quality of students' educational experience. Educational functions require practitioners to apply their indepth knowledge of theories in the real world of students with artistic mastery. Failure to address educational functioning is to argue against student affairs as a professional field. If practitioners do not make substantive contributions to students' educations, then the profession could best, and less expensively, be staffed by talented amateurs who have outgoing personalities and use good common sense. Successful educators in student affairs possess indepth understandings of student development and administrative/organizational theories that can be utilized to address the fundamental goals of the profession. Experienced, older professionals who are often from the common sense school of student affairs practice, generally hold the means for granting recognition and organizational rewards on many campuses. These older professionals may not value these kinds of activities to the extent that new professionals committed to the goals of intentional student development do. As a result, new professionals many times must be willing to undertake the educational functions for minimal extrinsic rewards.

An equally important mandate for the professional in student affairs is to evaluate the performance of the programs and services implemented with students. These evaluations should address questions about if and how students' behavior changed as a result of participation and whether one approach was more effective than some alternative or no intervention. Evaluations should employ psychometrically sound instruments and techniques such as well constructed interviews (Brown, 1979; Guba and Lincoln, 1981; Winston et. al., 1988). Asking participants, "Did you enjoy it?" or "Was this beneficial?" does not address the question of whether the intervention was effective. Such questions only address whether the students were entertained.

Finally, new professionals have a responsibility to contribute to the advancement of the profession through research that tests theory. Research, unlike evaluation, is seldom a primary job responsibility for most new professionals. It is something that professionals generally do in addition to the more clearly defined expectations. Consequently, most meaningful research will be the result of team efforts not isolated individual work. The team approach has several advantages: groups can divide the responsibilities and time demands into feasible units; teams allow for a pooling of skills and knowledge; team members can reinforce and encourage each other when competing demands become heavy; and the shared experience can improve *esprit d'corps* and can help cut across traditional departmental barriers.

On most campuses there are also persons available with expertise that may be lacking by a group of new professionals, such as statistical analyses or research design. Often senior professionals are quite willing to assist in studies, if asked. Psychology, counseling, higher education, or other academic departments usually have faculty members who are willing to consult on research projects. The faculty on university campuses that have good student personnel preparation programs can often contribute a knowledge of the major theories of student development and research strategies. These "experts" must be sought out; they will seldom seek out the new professional. Struggling with the issues raised by the paradigm shift and more traditional views of theory and research can be intellectually stimulating and, in the process, helps to distinguish the well-intentioned from the true professional.

Learning to achieve personal and professional balance is the principal task graduate students must first master as they become practicing professionals. How well new professionals gain theoretical and practical confidence and competence determines, in large measure, how successful they will ultimately be in the field and whether they will ever become professionals.

REFERENCES

American Council on Education. (1937, 1949). *The student personnel point of view.* Washington, D.C.: Author.

Argyris, C.; Putnam, R.; and Smith, D.M. (1987). *Action science: Concepts, methods, and skills for research and intervention.* San Francisco: Jossey-Bass Publishers.

Argyris, C., and Schon, D.A. (1978). *Theory in practice: Increasing professional effectiveness.* San Francisco: Jossey-Bass Publishers.

Blocher, D.H. (1987). On the uses and misuses of the term theory. *Journal of Counseling and Development,* 66, 67-68.

Brown, R.D. (1979). Key issues evaluating student affairs programs. In G.D. Kuh (Ed.), *Evaluation in student affairs* (pp. 13-31). Washington, D.C.: American College Personnel Association.

Caple, R.B. (1987a). The change process in developmental theory: A self-organization paradigm, part 1. *Journal of College Student Personnel,* 28, 4-11.

Caple, R.B. (1987b). The change process in developmental theory: A self-organization paradigm, part 2. *Journal of College Student Personnel,* 28, 100-04.

Carpenter, D.S.; Miller, T.K.; and Winston, R.B., Jr. (1980). Toward the professionalization of student affairs. *NASPA Journal,* 18(2), 16-22.

Chickering, A.W. (1969). *Education and identity.* San Francisco: Jossey-Bass Publishers.

Drum, D.J., and Lawler, A.C. (1988). *Developmental interventions: Theories, principles, and practices.* Columbus, Ohio: Merrill.

Guba, E.G., and Lincoln, Y.S. (1981). *Effective evaluation: Improving the usefulness of evaluation results through responsive and naturalistic approaches.* San Francisco: Jossey-Bass Publishers.

Heineman, D., and Strange, C. (1984). Uses of human development theory by entry-level practitioners in student affairs. *Journal of College Student Personnel,* 25(6), 528-33.

Hurst, J.C., and Jacobson, J.K. (1985). Theories underlying students' needs for programs. In M.J. Barr and L.A. Keating (Eds.), *Developing effective student services programs: Systematic approaches for practitioners* (pp. 109-36). San Francisco: Jossey-Bass Publishers.

Kohlberg, L. (1969). Stages and sequences: The cognitive-developmental approach to socialization. In D.P. Goslin (Ed.), *Handbook of socialization theory and research.* Chicago: Rand McNally.

Knefelkamp, L.L. (1984). The use of the Wells/Knefelkamp practice-to-theory-to-practice model. College Park, Maryland: University of Maryland. Unpublished manuscript.

Kuh, G.D.; Whitt, E.J.; and Shedd, J.D. (1987). *Student affairs work, 2001: A paradigmatic odyssey.* Alexandria, Virginia: American College Personnel Association.

Miller, T.K., and Prince, J.S. (1976). *The future of student affairs: A guide to student development in tomorrow's higher education.* San Francisco: Jossey-Bass Publishers.

Miller, T.K.; Winston, R.B., Jr.; and Mendenhall, W.R. (1983). Human development and higher education. In T.K. Miller, R.B. Winston, Jr., and W.R. Mendenhall (Eds.), *Administration and leadership in student affairs: Actualizing student development in higher education* (pp. 3-29). Muncie, Indiana: Accelerated Development.

Morrill, W.H.; Hurst, J.C.; and Oetting, E.R. (Eds.). (1980). *Dimensions of intervention for student development.* New York: Wiley and Sons.

Perry, W., Jr. (1970). *Forms of intellectual and ethical development in the college years: A scheme.* New York: Holt, Rinehart and Winston.

Rodgers, R.F. (1983). Using theory in practice. In T.K. Miller, R.B. Winston, Jr., and W.R. Mendenhall (Eds.), *Administration and leadership in student affairs: Actualizing student development in higher education* (pp. 111-44). Muncie, Indiana: Accelerated Development.

Rodgers, R.F., and Widick, C. (1980). Theory to practice: Uniting concepts, logic, and creativity. In F.B. Newton and K.L. Ender (Eds.), *Student development practices: Strategies for making a difference.* Springfield, Illinois: Charles C. Thomas Publisher.

Schon, D.A. (1987). *Educating the reflective practitioner: Toward a new design for teaching and learning in the professions.* San Francisco: Jossey-Bass Publishers.

Strange, C. (1981). Organizational barriers to student development. *NASPA Journal,* 19(1), 12-20.

Strange, C. (1983). Human development theory and administrative practice in student affairs: Ships passing in the daylight. *NASPA Journal,* 21(1), 2-8.

Thorngate, W. (1976). In general vs. it depends: Some comments on the Gergen-Schlenker debate. *Personality and Social Psychology Bulletin,* 2, 404-10.

Weick, K.E. (1979). *The social psychology of organizing* (2nd ed.). Reading, Massachusetts: Addison-Wesley.

Winston, R.B., Jr.; Bonney, W.C.; Miller, T.K.; and Dagley, J.C. (1988). *Promoting student development through intentionally structured groups: Principles, techniques, and applications.* San Francisco: Jossey-Bass Publishers.

Chapter 4

Developmental Concerns in Moving Toward Personal and Professional Competence

D. Stanley Carpenter

The notion of professional development can be considered a verb, an active process that cannot be taken for granted without risk. Such a view, however, runs counter to many often-espoused "accident" theories of career patterns or professional education. Indeed, student affairs professionals have traditionally valued experience and maturity over any kind of systematic learning. Graduate school is considered to be fine, to a point, but then one must get "out there" and discover reality. Practice does not make perfect, unless it is perfect practice. As the aphorism goes, ten years of experience is different from one year of experience ten times.

THE PROFESSION QUESTION

Student affairs may be a profession ". . . at least in practice . . . if not in theory . . ." (Trueblood, 1966, p. 80). In any case, professional attitudes, practice, and behavior are already expected of and achieved by practitioners (Stamatakos, 1987). According to the usual criteria, however, the field cannot be called a classic profession (Bloland, 1987; Komives, 1988;

Stamatakos, 1981, 1987). On the other hand, it has been argued that student affairs is an "emerging profession" (Carpenter, Miller, and Winston, 1980, p. 21). In any case, any position on the long-standing controversy in the literature does not make very much difference in the current context assuming that, "As individuals and as groups, we believe ourselves to be 'professionals,' and we believe our calling and colleagues with whom we work and with whom we have established formal organizations to be professional" (Stamatakos, 1981, p. 105).

Student affairs practitioners, then are expected to be professional and work in an environment that requires professionalism. In addition, student affairs as a field has attributes similar to those which are defined as a classic profession. The most important of such attributes for the present purposes is the existence of a professional community.

The Professional Community

A professional community may be thought of in terms of three sets of commonalities: shared goals and objectives, the existence of formal and informal sanctions, and attention to socialization and regeneration (Carpenter, 1983). For student affairs, the goal is full development of students' (and others) potential on college and university campuses. The sanctions take the form of accepted practices and, increasingly adherence to ethical codes. Socialization and regeneration concerns are reflected in preparation programs and continuing education, supervision, and mentoring activities at the work site and in regional and national settings. The existence of a student affairs professional community is acknowledged even by those who express doubt about the status of the field (Stamatakos, 1981).

If student affairs as a field is a professional community, then one can argue that human development principles can be applied to professional development just as they can in the larger community (Miller and Carpenter, 1980). This axiomatic assertion leads to five propositions (Miller and Carpenter, 1980, p. 84):

Proposition #1
Professional development is continuous and cumulative in

nature, moves from simpler to more complex behavior, and can be described via levels or stages held in common.

Proposition #2
Optimal professional development is a direct result of the interaction between the total person striving for positive professional growth and the environment.

Proposition #3
Optimal professional preparation combines mastery of a body of knowledge and a cluster of skills and competencies within the context of personal development.

Proposition #4
Professional credibility and excellence of practice are directly dependent upon the quality of professional preparation.

Proposition #5
Professional preparation is a lifelong learning process.

Proposition #1 implies the existence of professional developmental stages and four have been proposed (Miller and Carpenter, 1980) and supported by research (Carpenter and Miller, 1980; Wood, Winston, and Polkosnik, 1985): the Formative Stage, consisting of graduate and/or paraprofessional preparation; the Application Stage, encompassing beginning and intermediate practice and further preparation; the Additive Stage, involving intermediate to upper level practice and policy-making responsibility and increased professional sharing; and the Generative Stage, which spans upper level practice through retirement, and is attained in purest form by only a select few who influence the entire profession. For each of these stages, there are developmental tasks to be accomplished in identifiable (but not invariant) sequence, and failure to do so can lead to stagnation or decreased growth. The transitions from stage to stage are not always clear cut, but a little thought allows fairly simple classification.

The so-called new professional is generally in the early part of the Application Stage. Typically, he or she has negotiated some period of formal and informal initial preparation, most often a masters degree program and some paraprofessional experience, and has taken a first professional position. In any case, the new professional is now called upon to apply theories and suggestions in practical settings. The neophyte practitioner still needs a great deal of supervision and support and should get these things from some sort of mentor/mentee relationship(s) with one or more experienced professionals. In addition, the literature of the field and professional conferences on regional and national levels are good sources of help, encouragement, and guidance. The developmental imperative at this stage in a professional career is to move toward greater competence, confidence, and security. The person who succeeds in the first two or three years of practice will have the beginnings of a commitment to pursue a full career in student affairs. He/she will be in a position to make decisions about appropriate further preparation, whether academic (e.g., an advanced degree), on the job (taking a position of greater responsibility), or some combination of these.

If the new professional has entered student affairs from some other field of endeavor, he/she will be confronted with many of the developmental concerns of the Formative Stage. Such a person can "transfer" some learnings from the old setting to the new, but still will have some developmental catching up to do.

THE MILIEU OF STUDENT AFFAIRS— ENVIRONMENTAL CONTEXT

Having established a model for professional development which envisions an interaction with the environment, a consideration of the characteristics of that environment is in order. What is the nature of the career arena within which the new professional operates?

The Career Ladder

This section is based upon several studies of career patterns (Grant and Foy, 1972; Brooks and Avila, 1974; Paul and Hoover, 1980; Kuh, Evans, and Duke, 1983; Harder, 1983; Ostroth, Efrid, and Lerman, 1984; Burkhalter, 1984; Rickard, 1985), many conference presentations, and an interpretation of tacit knowledge in the student affairs field. The student affairs profession, unlike that of physicians, is not usually an object of aspiration until (and if) a person has entered college. Having had a positive (or perhaps a negative) experience in student activities or residence halls, some people choose to work in the field. Most often, they are guided to a masters preparation program and take on some paraprofessional position or internship/practicum. Upon graduation, such a person is ready for a first professional position, a two- or three-year "trial by fire." The new professional learns the ropes of student affairs work and either takes a more responsible position, returns to graduate school for an advanced degree, embarks on some combination of these two, or leaves the field altogether.

If this period of further preparation is productive, the next step (after some period in mid-level positions) is to take on a policy-level position, such as director or even chief student affairs officer (CSAO). At this point, the person makes decisions about taking on evermore increasing responsibilities by moving to larger schools or moving up hierarchically, or he or she may elect to stay in one position for a relatively long time. Professional counselors or faculty members may have arrived at their preferred levels at this stage, and never move again (or do so infrequently). Eventually, student affairs professionals either achieve or modify their career aspirations, complete their careers, and retire.

Attempting to capture thousands of career paths in two paragraphs is obviously folly. Clearly, variations on these themes are as numerous as the number of people in student affairs. What is important is that avenues for advancement and professional growth are identifiable.

Another consideration for new professionals is that there is a pyramid look to the career ladder. Each level of career advancement is composed of fewer positions than the preceding one— some number of entry-level jobs, a smaller number of mid-level positions and so on, with the number of CSAOs bounded by the number of college and universities (approximately 3,000). Further, people with no experience or background in student affairs are sometimes hired at each level (although this seems to be rarer now than in the past), even at the CSAO level.

Career ladder variability also must be considered in terms of practice setting. Major differences exist in any hypothesized path depending upon whether one prefers, for example, community colleges, small private colleges, regional state universities or colleges, or large research universities. Additionally, some professionals choose to make careers in specialized areas such as housing or financial aid, while some prefer central office work.

Constraints related to geographical preferences, dual career considerations, "stop out" periods for childbirth or rearing, stagnant economic or job market conditions, and many others must also be considered. For example, research indicating that CSAOs are staying in their positions longer and have more education and more experience than previously (Paterson, 1987) translates all the way down the line to a potential "aspirational logjam" (Carpenter, Guido-DiBrito, and Kelly, 1987, p. 8).

The intention here is not to frighten or depress, but to point out the necessity to be even more aware of professional development and excellence of practice in order to survive and thrive in a competitive environment. Many professionals choose not to compete, however, and either choose to leave or are forced out of student affairs at various career stages.

Leaving the Field: Negatives and Positives

Estimates of the proportion of student affairs professionals continuing to work in the field after five or six years vary from about two-thirds (Burns, 1982; Wood, Winston, and Polkosnik, 1985) to about two-fifths (Holmes, Verrier, and Chisholm, 1983). It is extremely difficult to get a true fix on this proportion because of methodological and definitional reasons, but it is undeniable that many people enter the field and then leave (Escott, 1976; Rickard, 1982). The question is why?

Some of the reasons are the same ones that affect the careers of those who stay in the field and were mentioned above. The relatively low number of positions at the top of the field compared to the entry level is discouraging to some who begin to perceive little chance for advancement (Bender, 1980). This job market problem interacts with personal developmental concerns such as dual career tension (Arnold, 1982) and geographical preferences or institutional loyalty (Burns, 1982). The differences between those who persist and those forced out by these and other variables are interesting to speculate about but, faced with similar circumstances, some people stay and some people go.

Stamatakos (1978) suggested that some professionals leave for reasons of their own, unrelated to the job market. Sometimes theory and reality (in the form of institutional agendas) conflict. New professionals may experience value conflicts between what they entered the field to do and what they actually do. If student contact and idealism were primary motivators for a student affairs career, and the new professional perceives that these things conflict with job expectations, especially at higher levels in the hierarchy, then disillusionment is likely. Such an occurrence is neither necessarily negative (for the field or the person), nor is it rare in other fields.

Relatedly, some people find that there is not a good fit between their preferred career reward structures and the field of student affairs. The work of Schein (1978) and DeLong (1981), in proposing the existence of career orientations and career anchors, is of interest in this context. DeLong (1981) discussed values and career needs in terms of career anchors, including technical competence, managerial competence, security, creativity, autonomy, identity, service, and variety. Wood, Winston, and Polkosnik (1985) found evidence that autonomy and geographical security orientations were related to attrition in student affairs and suggested further research into many other dimensions. High needs in some combination(s) of these career anchors could interact negatively with any given job setting or supervisory style, or even with perceptions of the field as a whole.

Burnout is another factor in attrition from student affairs. Some causes that have been identified for this syndrome are repetitive tasks, overextension, money issues, advancement issues, lack of challenge, politics, feedback and supervision issues, and lack of time for professional and personal development (Forney, Wallace-Schutzman, and Wiggers, 1982). Many of these causes apply to new professionals who are quite often called upon to work long hours under ambiguous direction for small salaries in the guise of paying their dues.

An important difference between burnout and the issues raised in previous paragraphs is that burnout is not part of a rational decision to change professions. Burnout is avoidable, whereas poorness of fit may not be.

Transferring Student Affairs Skills and Competencies to Other Settings

Recognizing the fact that some professionals leave student affairs at various career stages and for various reasons, Carpenter, Guido-DiBrito, and Kelly (1987) reviewed studies of competencies and skills fostered by student affairs preparation and practice, and compared them to indicators of success in business and management. They stated, "The field of student affairs demands varied and excellent management and communication skills, and these valuable talents are readily transferable to other fields of endeavor" (p. 12). The implication is that new professionals particularly are not "wasting" their time by trying out a career in student affairs because they gain good experience for the future whether their future is in the field or not. Hence, at the risk of rationalizing, the winnowing out process in student affairs may benefit both those who choose to persist and those who choose to leave.

The Importance of New Professionals

Student affairs needs a continuing supply of new professionals for many reasons. Changes in theory and research are most quickly communicated to the field and to practice by the most recently educated practitioners. New professionals bring vitality to student affairs organizations, and to college and university administrations generally. Further, new professionals are the first line of contact between students and the administration and people in such positions should be energetic and idealistic.

The attrition from the field that has been discussed at some length leads every year to vacancies for talented new professionals. The best situation for the profession would occur if the people who did not fit the field were the ones to leave it. Each new crop of professionals would be sorted, with the best continuing in the field and the others leaving the field. Clearly, no profession attains such an ideal, but a continuing pool of talent from which to draw is critical.

Again, the level of competition in the student affairs field implied by the pyramid of positions and other factors examined is rather daunting. Student affairs is not really different than many other fields. Competition exists for the favored slots in any business, and those who advance are the ones who pay the most attention to maximizing potential and competence. Professional development must be a systematic and intentional process.

IMPLICATIONS FOR INDIVIDUAL PROFESSIONAL DEVELOPMENT

Thus far, a case has been made that professional development is facilitated by an intentional awareness of the effects of professional context (described above) and personal development concerns (such as family orientation, the search for purpose in life, and many other things, the treatment of which is beyond the present scope). A model for professional development and socialization has been postulated in which the new professional is at the early Application Stage. The major focus of this period of a career is upon translating supervisor and environmental expectations and previous professional training (if any) into practical decisions while growing to be more autonomous. The new professional is accepting, adapting, and adopting the values of a new reference group, that of colleagues in the field, and is learning through apprenticeship those things that are most appropriately taught only by current practitioners (Caplow, 1964). Professional development activities can be structured with an adaptation (Carpenter, 1983) of Pavolko's (1971) profession-occupation continua.

Continuum #1: Knowledge of Theory and Levels of Skill

Now is not the time to stop learning! New professionals are often anxious to get "out there" and start applying the things they have learned about proper educational environments. This enthusiasm is laudable and can be harnessed to analyze the campus, the particular job setting, and the student clientele. Good questions include: What aspects of developmental theory are best suited to the students with whom I work? To what theoretical orientation do the student affairs staff at my institution subscribe? What practical skills do I need to augment (e.g., budgeting) to be successful and effective in my current setting and to make myself more valuable to the organization? In other words, the early years of practice can be used in developing a systematic learning paradigm that will be useful throughout a career.

Continuum #2: Clarification of Motivation and Relevance to Society

Many new professionals have only a nebulous idea of their motivations. Some may have entered the field to generically "help" students. By the time they take their first professional position (if they have any formal training), this idealism will be augmented by some good ideas but reality will soon intervene. Professionals who practice within organizations (e.g., physicians in hospitals) often have to make adjustments to their professional values in order to conform with legitimate organizational goals. The new professional should work toward an informed and practical idealism, avoid fighting battles that cannot be won, and guard against building up resentment and frustration. The successful student affairs practitioner is one who has developed a healthy attitude toward the difficulty of managing educational environments without losing enthusiasm and commitment.

Continuum #3: Decisions Regarding Preparation and Career

As discussed above, the most important decision for the new professional is often whether to continue past the first position. However, an equally important consideration is the development of a professional attitude that will color the career, regardless of its length. The same set of learnings will serve both ends. The new professional needs to carefully analyze reactions and preferences throughout the first job in order to understand whether any discomfort or employment related unhappiness is rooted in the specific work setting or in a goodness of fit problem related to the practice of student affairs work. Working conditions may be very different in specialty areas such as housing and financial aid, and will certainly vary from campus to campus and even within the same university or college. For these reasons as well as in the service of intentional development, the new professional should spend time interacting with many different practitioners. Perceptions need to be examined and balanced against the opinions of trusted colleagues. Important also is gaining a more sophisticated understanding of the professional job market and the things required to succeed in the field. If advanced education and skills are likely to be needed, the young professional should become aware of this and take steps to get them. After two or three years in a first position, most new professionals will wish to change jobs. This second job should be carefully chosen with regard to institutional setting, level of responsibility, area of practice, and many other variables. Only through continual research can these and similar decisions be made properly.

Continuum #4: Autonomy of Professional Behavior
Autonomy is a critical dimension involving the very essence of professionalism. No matter what the level of preparation prior to the first professional position, one naturally conforms to the expectations of the institutional environment and especially the supervisor for some period of time as a "safety net." Learning to cut the umbilical cord and make decisions independently can be tricky. Often entry-level positions do not allow for a great deal of flexibility in practice. New professionals will frequently be given more latitude, however, as they demonstrate competence and confidence. The key is to be willing to try new things and take initiative without worrying unduly about making mistakes. Mistakes will be made unless nothing is being accom-

plished. Under ideal conditions, these mistakes can be mined for new learning and not dealt with punitively. One thing that is helpful is to study and discuss the successes and failures of colleagues. Developing professional judgment is a trial-and-error process for which there are few shortcuts. The best way to become autonomous is to act autonomously and deal with the results.

Continuum #5: Developing a Sense of Professional Community
Not surprisingly, learning to take a place in the professional community is important. In the early part of the career, new professionals begin to think of themselves as student affairs professionals and represent themselves as such to the campus community and to students. The new professional has a wealth of resources available for the asking (or finding) in the form of professional associations, publications, and presentations. Learning about the various professional associations in the student affairs field and assessing their individual strengths is important. Critical also is developing colleague relationships on the home campus and across the region and nation, for many of the reasons detailed above. Gaining the respect and friendship of colleagues leads to an increasingly sophisticated understanding of the values of the profession as well as a host of new ideas about how to do one's job.

Continuum #6: Activities Related to Professional Publications
The professional literature deserves heavy emphasis because informed judgment is what separates the practitioner-scholar from the technician. The point of the professional literature is to aid in developing an opinion. This opinion will ideally be derived from a careful consideration of what has been published on the subject at hand, an evaluation of the quality of individual sources, and some judgment about relevance and applicability to a specific setting or circumstance. Most masters programs make a nod in this direction, but few do much more. The new professional should read voraciously and constantly and begin to decide which sources (journals, newsletters, periodicals) have the most to offer. Every phase of professional practice from the most esoteric theoretical considerations to the most mundane program-

ming ideas will be strengthened by a conscious determination to keep up-to-date. The literature is a record of the critical transactions of the professional community. Without consistent input, the Application Stage professional soon has very little to apply.

The other half of a professional use of the literature is the responsibility to contribute. New professionals often feel they have nothing to offer and are intimidated by the publication or presentation process. As in all phases of development, this process should be continuous and cumulative and move from simpler to more complex levels. That is, the only way to learn to publish is to try to publish. Again (with emphasis), professional sharing is not an option, but rather an affirmative obligation. As an example of professionalism, consider a physician who developed the cure to some abhorrent disease. He/she would not think of withholding the treatment from the medical community for competitive advantage or because of laziness or excuses. Similarly, student affairs professionals should not fail to share their best thinking with one another.

Continuum #7: Developing a Sense of Ethical Practice
Just as there is seldom only one best way to accomplish student affairs program objectives, some measure of disagreement is not unusual with regard to ethical decision making. The well-prepared new professional will have some idea of ethical codes and their importance, but only a rudimentary concept of their application. If, for any reason, the new professional is unfamiliar with the ethical standards for a particular practice setting, action should be taken immediately to remediate this deficiency. A good role to follow initially is that if some practice or action seems questionable, then ask the question. Early in the career, the new professional should develop the habit of discussing with supervisors and peers the ethical consequences of various decisions. The literature will often add insight and substance to these debates and a sensitivity to potential organization/practitioner/client conflicts will help the new professional contribute to policy discussions and figure out the "rules" for ethical practice.

CONCLUSION

Professional development does not just happen, it must be structured and intentionally enhanced. A community exists in student affairs, a shared culture, which one ignores at the risk of personal and professional inadequacy. No pretense is made that this brief treatment (or, indeed, this entire book) is anything more than a starting place for the serious new professional. Many paths to excellence and professionalism are available; on each, the tasks are daunting but not impossible. The key is to make the best choices possible, evaluate those choices, make more choices, and so on. As a guide, keep in the mind the title of Buckminster Fuller's (1970) book, *I Seem to be a Verb*.

REFERENCES

Arnold, K. (1982). Career development for the experienced student affairs professional. *NASPA Journal*, 20(2), 3-8.

Bender, B.E. (1980). Job market satisfaction in student affairs. *NASPA Journal*, 18(2), 2-9.

Bloland, P.A. (1987, March). Are we a profession? Paper presented at the joint national conference of the American College Personnel Association and the National Association of Student Personnel Administrators, Chicago, Illinois.

Brooks, G., and Avila, J. (1974). The chief student personnel administrator and his staff: A profile. *NASPA Journal*, 11(4), 41-47.

Burkhalter, J.P. (1984). Career patterns of chief student personnel administrators. (Doctoral dissertation, University of Georgia, 1984). Dissertation Abstracts International, 45, 425A.

Burns, M.A. (1982). Who leaves the student affairs field? *NASPA Journal*, 20(2), 9-12.

Caplow, T. (1964). *The sociology of work*. New York: McGraw-Hill.

Carpenter, D.S. (1983). The student affairs profession: A developmental perspective. In T.K. Miller, R.B. Winston, Jr., and W.R. Mendenhall (Eds.), *Administration and leader-*

ship in student affairs: Actualizing student development in higher education (pp. 146-65). Muncie, Indiana: Accelerated Development.

Carpenter, D.S.; Guido-DiBrito, F.; and Kelly, J.P. (1987). Transferability of student affairs skills and competencies: Light at the end of the bottleneck. *NASPA Journal,* 24(3), 7-14.

Carpenter, D.S., and Miller, T.K. (1981). An analysis of professional development in student affairs work. *NASPA Journal,* 19(1), 2-11.

Carpenter, D.S.; Miller, T.K.; and Winston, R.B. (1980). Toward the professionalization of student affairs. *NASPA Journal,* 18(2), 16-22.

DeLong, T.J. (1981). Career anchors: A new concept in career development for the professional educator. Paper presented at the annual meeting of the American Educational Research Association, Los Angeles, California (ERIC Document Reproduction Service No. ED 209 545).

Escott, S.B. (1976). Anatomy of a placement cotillion. *NASPA Journal,* 14(1), 40-52.

Forney, D.S.; Wallace-Schutzman, F.; and Wiggers, T.T. (1982). Burnout among career development professionals: Preliminary findings and implications. *Personnel and Guidance Journal,* 60, 435-39.

Fuller, B.R. (1970). *I seem to be a verb.* New York: Bantam Books.

Grant, W.H., and Foy, J. (1972). Career patterns of student personnel administrators. *NASPA Journal,* 10(2), 106-13.

Harder, M.B. (1983). Career patterns of chief student personnel administrators. *Journal of College Student Personnel,* 24, 443-48.

Holmes, D.; Verrier, D.; and Chisholm, P. (1983). Persistence in student affairs work: Attitudes and job shifts among master's program graduates. *Journal of College Student Personnel,* 24, 438-43.

Komives, S.R. (1988, March). The art of becoming professional. Paper presented at the annual conference of the American CollegePersonnel Association, Miami, Florida.

Kuh, G.D.; Evans, N.J.; and Duke, A. (1983). Career paths and responsibilities of chief student affairs officers. *NASPA Journal* 21(1), 39-47.

Miller, T.K., and Carpenter, D.S. (1980). Professional preparation for today and tomorrow. In D.G. Creamer (Ed.), *Student development in higher education: Theories, practices, and future directions.* Washington, D.C.: American College Personnel Association.

Ostroth, D.D.; Efrid, F.D.; and Lerman, L.S. (1984). Career patterns of chief student affairs officers. *Journal of College Student Personnel,* 25(5), 443-47.

Paterson, B.G. (1987). An examination of the professional status of chief student affairs officers. *College Student Affairs Journal,* 8(1), 13-20.

Paul, W.L., and Hoover, R.E. (1980). Chief student personnel administrator: A decade of change. *NASPA Journal,* 18(1), 33-39.

Pavalko, R.M. (1971). *Sociology of occupations and professions.* Itasca, Illinois: F.E. Peacock.

Rickard, S.T. (1982). Turnover at the top: A study of the chief student affairs officer. *NASPA Journal,* 20(2), 35-41.

Rickard, S.T. (1985). Titles of student affairs officers: Institutional autonomy or professional standardization? *NASPA Journal,* 23(2), 44-49.

Schein, E.H. (1978). *Career dynamics: Matching individual and organizational need.* Reading, Massachusetts: Addison-Wesley.

Stamatakos, L.C. (1978). Unsolicited advice for new professionals. *Journal of College Student Personnel,* 19, 325-29.

Stamatakos, L.C. (1981). Student affairs progress toward professionalism: Recommendations for action. *Journal of College Student Personnel,* 22(2), 105-13 and 22(3), 197-205.

Stamatakos, L.C. (1987, March). Are we a profession? Paper presented at the joint national conference of the American College Personnel Association and the National Association of Student Personnel Administrators. Chicago, Illinois.

Trueblood, D.L. (1966). The educational preparation of the college student personnel leader of the future. In G.J. Klopf (Ed.), *College student personnel in the years ahead.* Washington, D.C.: American College Personnel Association.

Wood, L.; Winston, R.B.; and Polkosnik, M.C. (1985). Career orientations and professional development of young student affairs professionals. *Journal of College Student Personnel,* 26, 532-39.

Chapter 5

A Lifestyle Approach to Stress Management

Frances O'Brien and Steven K. Erwin

Society rewards hard work and dedication. Those who are highly committed to this aspect of their lives are putting in extra hours and reaping the benefits. However, these professionals may be neglecting their personal health and well-being because the current focus on holistic health, or wellness, encourages individuals to balance the dimensions of their lives.

The student affairs professional can avoid an imbalance by adopting and practicing effective lifestyle decision making and stress management. Positive lifestyle choices can increase the quality of life. However, the new professional's lifestyle is often characterized by negative variables such as work overload, an inability to refuse projects, and neglect of social commitments. The resulting stress has an impact on the quality of relationships and job performance.

Stressors

Examining effective stress management requires a definition of the terms *stress* and *stressors*. Stress describes the physiological reaction that occurs when an individual perceives something as causing mental tension. Stressors are the stimuli that cause stress.

Seyle (1976, p. 51) outlined several potential stressors that may be encountered by new professionals:

- *Questioning position status and prestige.* Status and prestige may be equated with salary and responsibility levels, scope of decision-making power, and position in the hierarchy.
- *Balancing professionalism with personal lifestyle.* Role modeling of inappropriate lifestyle choices (involving certain social activities or developing personal relationships) will likely be scrutinized.
- *Planning a career and goal setting.* Internal and external pressures affect advancement and career progression. Aspirations for rapid advancement are tempered by the realism of limited mid-level opportunities, inadequate skills development for advancement, or unrealistic goals.
- *Assessing progress and accountability.* Supervisors set expectations and evaluate progress. The new professional must be responsible to avoid pitfalls and undesirable outcomes.
- *Maintaining motivation.* Motivated and energetic individuals experience periods of low motivation which may correspond with periods of low work and time demands. In contrast, low motivation at a time of increased demands may lead to considerable difficulty.
- *Handling political and economic issues.* New professionals sometimes lack the instinct or knowledge to effectively deal with the realities of campus politics and economics that exist within and between institutional factions such as faculty, administration, and alumni.
- *Evaluating intrinsic/extrinsic compensation.* Extrinsic rewards (salary/benefits) in student affairs sometimes fall below what peers receive in other professions. In contrast, there are considerable intrinsic rewards such as a sense of accomplishment from contributing to student success and personal growth. The dilemma is in evaluating and making decisions based on extrinsic and intrinsic rewards.
- *Evaluating opprtunities/desire for advancement.* Student affairs offers several opportunities which contain possible hidden pitfalls. The new professional may lack clarity in determining which institutions offer the best or safest opportunities, in

detecting problem-solving situations prior to entering a new position, and in preparing for advancement.
- *Lacking a peer group.* The abrupt entry-level transition and mobile nature of the student affairs profession allows only short time for developing personal and professional relationships.
- *Competing with peers.* Excessive competition and decreased cooperation with peers leads to cynicism that may contribute to an unhealthy and unproductive work environment. In contrast, a lack of competition promotes acceptance of less than excellent performance standards and little *espirit de corps*.
- *Translating theory into practice.* A solid theoretical understanding does not necessarily translate into effective program implementation.
- *Varying schedule and time demands.* Availability for students and colleagues is one key ingredient to success. Many positions demand long hours and a varied schedule.
- *Feeling instable.* The ability to "put down roots" and feel a sense of belonging to a community is affected by the transient nature of entry-level student affairs positions.

BEGINNING EFFECTIVE STRESS MANAGEMENT

New professionals can begin to effectively manage stress by identifying key sources of personal stress and continuing with consistent implementation of proper stress management techniques. Common phrases such as "I'll do something for myself when I'm finished with this project" or "I can handle this" illustrate the tendency for selectivity and avoidance of implementation.

Stress is typically caused by three variables: threat, change, and uncertainty. The variables do not have to be real, an individual can perceive them as real. According to McLean (1979), "It is immaterial whether the agent [stress-producing activity] of the situation we face is unpleasant or pleasant; all that counts is the intensity of the demand for readjustment or adaptation" (p. 35). Therefore, a pleasant situation such as receiving an award or being promoted can also cause stress.

Self-esteem and attitude also affect an individual's perception and response to different stimuli, events, and situations. People react to situations in different ways. They are also more objective and positive in their assessment of stimuli when they feel good about themselves.

In contrast, low self-esteem or poor attitude promotes unhealthy, negative and critical perceptions about life's events. Clearly, self-esteem and attitude are important in the way one views career activities and affiliations. New professionals respond in a healthy manner when they perceive that they are valued by their institution.

Eliminating Stress

In managing stress, do not try to eliminate stress entirely. Stress is an adaptive response allowing increased energy and arousal to deal with increased demands and stimuli (Giordiano and Everly, 1979, p. 126). Only when the physical response goes beyond being adaptive does stress become harmful.

Walter Cannon's expression, "fight or flight response" (Henry and Ely, 1980, p. 82), is often used interchangeably with the stress response. The body gears up to fight or flee from the threatening situation. In a less complicated society, the "fight or flight response" is very adaptive. The individual confronts the stimulus or runs to avoid it and the situation is temporarily resolved.

In our complex society, however, individuals are confronted with situations that they perceive as threatening but are not suited to a "fight or flight response." A threatening situation at work is a prime example. Time is needed for adjustment, yet the body still gears up for an immediate "fight or flight response." The stress response becomes maladaptive when the body is constantly excited and does not have the means or ability to reduce stress. Constant arousal, without a means to restore the system's equilibrium, leads to harmful effects of stress.

Occupational Stress

A common mistake is to equate occupational stress with the number of hours an individual works. Although long hours can cause stress, there is not a causal relationship between the two. Individuals can work long hours every day and be relaxed if they enjoy their work. Conversely, an individual can work only a few hours a day and encounter tremendous stress. Although stressors are individually defined, there are some occupational stressors that appear to surface regularly. According to Kovacek (1983), the following occupational stressors are fairly common among student affairs professionals: role ambiguity/rigidity, role conflicts, work overload or stagnation, exccessive or inadequate responsibilities, and change.

Role Ambiguity/Rigidity

"One of the oldest subjectively defined occupational stress variables is role ambiguity (Holt, 1982, p. 425). Role ambiguity refers to having too little direction. Too little direction or structure may lead to individual uncertainty concerning job performance and wasted time or confusion. The result is that an individual spends more time determining others' expectations than actually working.

In contrast, role rigidity refers to having too much structure. For example, a new professional with little latitude in work structure becomes concerned with perfection or deviating from the structure and ultimately feels threatened by the controlling nature of the job.

Role Conflicts

Role conflicts arise for many reasons and can create considerable stress. The reasons may include having more than one supervisor, having roles within an organization that conflict, or having divided loyalties among superiors, peers, and subordinates. The resulting uncertainty can cause job stress. A common example of role stress is when pressure to work late conflicts with family or social needs.

Work Overload and Stagnation
Work overload refers to an imbalance between the work expected and the time required to perform the job. Work overload often leads to a fear of failure as the new professional produces unsatisfactory results in keeping pace. Performance may be threatening for those who have high standards.

Work stagnation produces a similar feeling of dissatisfaction if individuals feel understimulated or unchallenged. Levi (1981) highlighted this point when he stated, "People have psychological requirements from their work other than those specified in a contract for employment. Two such requirements are that the job be reasonably demanding and there are opportunities to learn" (p. 124).

Excessive/Inadequate Responsibilities
The stress created from having excessive responsibility is more obvious than stress created from inadequate responsibilities. Excessive responsibility may force people to give less attention to certain areas. This often leads to a threat or fear of failure. Excessive responsibility becomes a problem if individuals are held responsible for things they cannot control. It may cause some individuals to feel inadequate or overwhelmed, waiting in fear of being discovered or exposed as frauds. Whereas, inadequate responsibilities may create stress through underutilization of talents and may stem the flow of personal energy and professional talents. These responsibilities also encourage a "Why bother?" attitude which ultimately produces stress when personal and professional aspirations exceed available opportunities.

Change
Change is another variable that typically causes stress. According to Benson (1975, p. 56), "Change, whether for good or bad, causes stress to human beings." Job relocation is a good example of change. "Relocation is a regular and increasing phenomenon [in student affairs] that subjects employees and their families to stress that may be severe, debilitating, or chronically disabling"

(Warshaw, 1979, p. 140). By minimizing other changes during a job transition, the potential stress can be diminished.

Woodburn (1985) reported that the imposter syndrome is fairly common, especially when adjusting to a new and unfamiliar job. Woodburn (1985, p. 72) stated that as much as 40 percent of successful career people feel that they are professionally inadequate. In addition, nearly three-fourths of all people have felt like imposters at least once in their lives. Woodburn also stated that victims of the imposter syndrome can become anxiety junkies, worried that eventually they will be discovered. The despair they feel is usually unwarranted. Needless to say, new professionals who feel they are "faking it" are not alone.

Occupational Coping Strategies

For many career-oriented professionals, job responsibilities become a way of affirming one's self and position in society. Considering the new professional's job status, the occupational dimension is a natural starting point for developing strategies for coping with stress. An individual can alter certain work behaviors and portions of the work environment to modify exposure to potential stressors. This alteration is referred to by Giordiano and Everly (1979, p. 125) as "social engineering." The essence is to seek alternatives or modify one's position in relation to the stressors.

An initial step in minimizing occupational stress is to ensure that one's career is in line with personal values and interests. Individuals searching for a job must accurately represent skills and experience to potential employers. Once a job is located, they must attempt to understand the functional responsibilities, lines of accountability, and method of evaluation. Managing these areas will not necessarily eliminate occupational stress but will certainly reduce role ambiguity and related problems.

As noted previously, success in the student affairs profession is often linked to change and transition (variables that can cause stress). One strategy, when faced with a major change, is to minimize other life changes. More specifically, maintain social supports, healthy eating habits and sleeping behavior, and physical and leisure activity.

Personal/Professional Balance Strategies

The inability to separate personal and professional roles contributes greatly to stress. To completely separate these two areas and define each exclusively is difficult. No matter how hard an attempt is made to make the distinction, some overlap is bound to occur. Minimizing overlap is effective in most cases. For example, if a personal issue arises, the stressor can be minimized by initiating action, resolution, and/or closure. The individual has reduced the personal stress through action and focus on work. The same strategy could be helpful in eliminating professional stressors at work to avoid carrying them over to personal time. The key for new professionals in balancing personal and professional roles begins with an attempt to balance the physical, emotional, intellectual, spiritual, and social dimensions of their lives.

Physical Health Strategies

Proper physical health results from a balance of activity and nutrition. Both are instrumental in maintaining a healthy lifestyle. Aerobic exercise is one of the most effective activities in helping to reduce the effects of stress. The key to aerobic exercise, which focuses on elevating and maintaining heart rate, is for new professionals to find an activity that they enjoy and make time to regularly engage in that activity. Examples of aerobic exercise include jogging, swimming, brisk walking, biking, aerobic dance, and cross-country skiing.

"Proper nutrition means that all essential nutrients—that is, carbohydrates, fats, protein, vitamins, minerals, and water—are supplied and utilized in adequate balance to maintain optimal health and well-being" (Kirschmann, 1975, p. 1). Physical health and performance are affected when a person does not get the proper nutritional intake. Without adequate exercise and nutrition, the body is more susceptible to illness and the effects of stress.

Emotional Coping Strategies

Everyone experiences emotion. Spontaneous expression of emotions is both healthy and appropriate within certain social parameters. By acknowledging feelings and emotions, new professionals can cope with them in a more adaptive manner and help reduce the ill-effects of excessive stress. Society, however, tends to reinforce predictability and consistency with regard to feelings and emotions. Until people feel comfortable expressing their feelings and emotions, they will continue to experience the anxiety and stress that often accompany nonexpression.

Mental/Intellectual Coping Strategies

Fitness is a state of motion and a state of mind. Because of the relationship between the mind and the body, a healthy mind is a prerequisite for optimal health. A balanced lifestyle can also be maintained through intellectual stimulation as a new professional keeps up-to-date on happenings within student affairs. This involves such professional development activities as reading journals, attending conferences, participating in staff development programs, studying technological changes, and furthering formal education. Intellectual stimulation also involves accepting professional challenges by broadening job responsibilities or organizational involvements.

Spiritual Strategies

The spiritual dimension explores the meaning of life and personal perceptions of life. When individuals feel that their lives have meaning, they are more inclined to experience satisfaction. If personal behaviors are inconsistent with personal values, an individual can become confused, uncertain, and unbalanced.

The meaning of human existence can be defined through values clarification and the consideration of morality, mortality, and cultural norms. What things in life are important to us and why? For the new professional in student affairs, satisfaction with personal spirituality may prove beneficial in meetings with students who are wrestling with spiritual issues. However, role modeling without a clear sense of values and congruency between personal behaviors and beliefs is difficult.

Social Strategies
Humans are social beings by nature. Strengthening contacts with family, friends, and colleagues helps to satisfy social needs. Maintaining social contacts is particularly important during periods of stress because of the support and acceptance received. When individuals feel loved and needed, they are more inclined to feel better about themselves. During stressful periods, the assurance that a person is valued can help in maintaining a much healthier perspective on life.

CONCLUSION

The goal of effective stress management is positive physical and mental health. However, student affairs professionals tend to demonstrate selectivity or avoidance in implementing effective stress management techniques. Random attempts at stress management will yield a less than satisfactory result.

Effective stress management is a lifelong process consisting of proper self-assessment, planning and implementation. The benefits of proactive stress management include: increased job satisfaction, enhanced professional development, improved personal health, heightened self-esteem, and greater performance effectiveness.

As with any portion of a holistic health (wellness) model, stress management is a matter of personal choice. Positive lifestyle choices involve personal satisfaction and decision making, as well as recognizing responsibilities and accepting the consequences of personal choices. Longevity and quality of life will be greatly enhanced for those who learn to manage day-to-day stressors.

REFERENCES

Benson, H. (1975). *The relaxation response.* New York: Avon Books.

Giordiano, D., and Everly, G. (1979). *Controlling stress and tension: A holistic approach.* Englewood Cliffs, New Jersey: Prentice-Hall.

Henry, J.P., and Ely, D.L. (1980). Ethological and physiological theories. In I. Kutash; L. Schlesinger; and Associates (Eds.), *Handbook on stress and anxiety* (p. 82). San Francisco: Jossey-Bass Publishers.

Holt, R.R. (1982). Occupational stress. In L. Goldberger and S. Bresznitz (Eds.), *Handbook on stress: Theoretical and clinical aspects* (p. 425). New York: The Free Press.

Kirschmann, J.D. (1975). *Nutrition almanac* (rev. ed). New York: McGraw-Hill.

Kovacek, P.R. (1983). Stress stoppers: Managing stress effectively. Detroit, Michigan: Henry Ford Hospital.

Levi, L. (1981). *Preventing work stress.* Reading, Massachusetts: Addison-Wesley Publishing Company.

McLean, A.A. (1979). *Work stress.* Reading, Massachusetts: Addison-Wesley Publishing Company.

Seyle, H. (1976). *The stress of life.* New York: McGraw-Hill.
Warshaw, L.J. (1979). *Managing stress.* Reading, Massachusetts: Addison-Wesley Publishing Company.

Woodburn, J. (1985, March). Faking it. *Milwaukee Magazine,* 125, 71-76.

Appendix

A Resource Guide for New Professionals and Supervisors in Student Affairs

This appendix is compiled as a resource guide for developing professional involvement and knowledge. Some of the associations and journals listed are specific to functional areas within student affairs such as housing, orientation, and admissions. Others encompass larger student affairs interests. It is hoped that this resource list will satisfy your professional interests and needs.

American Association for Counseling and Development (AACD)
5999 Stevenson Avenue
Alexandria, VA 22304
(703) 823-9800
Guidepost, Journal of Counseling and Development

American Association for Higher Education (AAHE)
One Dupont Circle, Suite 600
Washington, D.C. 20036
(202) 293-6440
The AAHE Bulletin, Change Magazine

American Association of Collegiate Registrars and Admissions
    Officers (AACRAO)
One Dupont Circle, Suite 330
Washington, D.C. 20036
(202) 293-9161
AACRAO Data Dispenser

American Association of Community and Junior Colleges
    (AACJC)
621 Duke Street
Alexandria, VA 22314
(703) 293-7050
Community and Junior College Journal

American College Personnel Association (ACPA)
5999 Stevenson Avenue
Alexandria, VA 22304
(703) 823-9800
Journal of College Student Development

American Council on Education (ACE)
One Dupont Circle, Suite 800
Washington, D.C. 20036
(202) 939-9300
Educational Record, Higher and National Affairs Newsletter

Association for Continuing Education
1700 Asp Avenue
Norman, OK 73037
(404) 325-1021
Continuing Higher Education

Association for Counselor Education and Supervision (ACES)*
% Thomas Hosie
Coordinator of Counselor Education
Louisiana State University
Baton Rouge, LA 79803
(504) 388-2202
Journal of Counselor Education and Supervision

Association of College and University Housing Officers—
   International (ACUHO-I)
Jones Tower, Suite 140
101 Curl Drive
Columbus, OH 43210-1195
(614) 292-0099
ACUHO-I Journal, Talking Stick Newsletter

Association of College Unions—International (ACU-I)
400 E. Seventh Street
Bloomington, IN 47405
(812) 332-8017
*The Bulletin of the Association of College Unions—
   International*

Association of University and College Counseling Center
   Directors (AUCCCD)
Counseling Center
University of Wisconsin—Stevens Point
Stevens Point, WI 54481
(715) 346-3553

Association on Handicapped Student Services Programs in
   Post-secondary Education
AHSSPPE Business Office
P.O. Box 21192
Columbus, OH 43221
(614) 488-4972
Journal of Postsecondary Education and Disability

College Placement Council, Inc. (CPC)
62 Highland Avenue
Bethlehem, PA 18017
(215) 868-1421
Journal of College Placement

National Academic Advising Association (NACADA)*
c/o Peggy King
Assistant Dean of Student Development
Schenectady County Community College
78 Washington Avenue
Schednectady, NY 12305
(518) 346-6211

National Association for Campus Activities (NACA)
P.O. Box 6828
Columbia, SC 29260
(803) 782-7121
Programming Magazine

National Association for Women Deans, Administrators, and Counselors (NAWDAC)
1625 I Street, NW
Washington, DC 20016
(202) 659-9330
NAWDAC Journal

National Association of College and University Business Officers (NACUBO)
One Dupont Circle, Suite 500
Washington, DC 20036
(202) 861-2500
The Business Officer

National Association of College and University Chaplains and Directors of Residence Life
Ohio Wesleyan University
61 South Sandusky
Delaware, OH 43015
(614) 369-4431

National Association of Independent Colleges and Universities (NAICU)
1717 Massachusetts Avenue, NW, Suite 503
Washington, DC 20036
(202) 387-7623
NAICU News

National Association of Student Financial Aid Administrators (NASFAA)
1920 L Street, NW
Washington, DC 20036
(202) 785-0453
Journal of Student Financial Aid

National Association of Student Personnel Administrators (NASPA)
1700 18th Street, NW, Suite 301
Washington, DC 20009
(202) 265-7500
NASPA Journal, NASPA Forum

National Clearinghouse for Commuter Programs (NCCP)
1195 Stamp Union
University of Maryland
College Park, MD 20742
(301) 454-5274
The Commuter

National Council on Student Development (NCSD)
AACJC, One Dupont Circle
Suite 410
Washington, DC 20036
(202) 293-7050

National Intramural Recreation Sports Association (NIRSA)
221 Gill Coliseum
Oregon State University
Carvallis, OR 97331
(503) 737-2088
The NIRSA Journal

National Orientation Directors Association (NODA)*
% Raymond Passkiewicz
Davenport College
4123 West Main Street
Kalamazoo, MI 49009
(616) 382-2835
NODA Journal

National University Continuing Education Association
    (NUCEA)
One Dupont Circle, Suite 615
Washington, DC 20036
(202) 659-3130

*Denotes address, as of January 1990, which may change when president of organization changes.

NASPA Publications
ORDER FORM

	Quantity	Cost
The New Professional: A Resource Guide for New Student Affairs Professionals and Their Supervisors. Monograph Series No. 10, February 1990. $7.95 members, $9.95 nonmembers	____	____
From Survival to Success: Promoting Minority Student Retention. Monograph Series No. 9, December 1988. $7.95 members, $9.95 nonmembers	____	____
Student Affairs and Campus Dissent. Monograph Series No. 8, March 1988 $5.95 members, $7.50 nonmembers	____	____
Alcohol Policies and Procedures on College and University Campuses. Monograph Series No. 7, July 1987. $5.95 members, $7.50 nonmembers	____	____
Opportunities for Student Development in Two-Year Colleges. Monograph Series No. 6, October 1986. $5.95 members, $7.50 nonmembers	____	____
Private Dreams, Shared Visions: Student Affairs Work in Small Colleges. Monograph Series No. 5, April 1986. $5.95 members, $7.50 nonmembers	____	____

	Quantity	Cost
Promoting Values Development in College Students. Monograph Series No. 4, October 1985. $5.95 members, $7.50 nonmembers	____	____
Translating Theory into Practice: Implications of Japanese Management Theory for Student Personnel Administrators. Monograph Series No. 3, March 1985. $5.95 members, $7.50 nonmembers	____	____
Risk Management and the Student Affairs Professional. Monograph Series No. 2, June 1984. $5.95 members, $7.50 nonmembers	____	____
Career Perspectives in Student Affairs. Monograph Series No. 1, January 1984. $5.95 members, $7.50 nonmembers	____	____
Points of View. $5 members, $7 nonmembers	____	____
Issues and Perspectives on Academic Integrity. $1 members, $1.50 nonmembers	____	____
NASPA Journal. $35 annual subscription, $9.50 single copy. If single issue, indicate volume and issue: _____	____	____
TOTAL	____	____

Please return completed form with check, money order, institutional purchase order, or credit card authorization. Return to: NASPA, 1700 18th Street, NW, Suite 301, Washington, D.C. 20009-2508; (202) 265-7500.

Payment enclosed ☐   P.O. enclosed ☐   Bill my credit card ☐

VISA ☐   MasterCard ☐   Expiration Date _____

Account Number _____   Signature _____

Please print

Name _____   NASPA Membership ID No. _____

Institution _____

Address _____

City _____   State _____   Zip _____